where to go when

where to go when

UNFORGETTABLE TRIPS FOR EVERY MONTH

Penguin
Random
House

Contributors Steph Dyson,
Taraneh Ghajar Jerven, Rebecca Hallett,
Stephen Keeling, Mike MacEacheran,
Shafik Meghji, Olivia Rawes, Daniel
Stables, Gavin Thomas, Aimee White

Senior Editor Alison McGill
Senior Designer Laura O'Brien
Project Editor Lucy Richards
Project Art Editor Ben Hinks
Fact-checkers Edward Aves, Emma
Gibbs, Tim Hannigan, Georgia Stephens
Editors Danielle Watt, Rebecca Flynn,
Emma Grundy Haigh, Lucy Sara-Kelly
US Executive Editor Lori Hand
US Editor Jennette ElNaggar
Proofreader Kathryn Glendenning
Indexer Hilary Bird
Additional Picture Research
Harriet Whitaker
Senior Cartographic Editor
Casper Morris
Jacket Designers Laura O'Brien,
Ben Hinks
Senior DTP Designer Jason Little
Senior Producer Stephanie McConnell
Managing Editor Hollie Teague
Art Director Maxine Pedliham
Publishing Director Georgina Dee

This American Edition, 2019
First American Edition, 2007
Published in the United States by DK Publishing
1450 Broadway, Suite 801, New York, NY 10018
Copyright © 2007, 2019 Dorling Kindersley Limited
DK, a Division of Penguin Random House LLC
014–314556–Oct/2019
21 22 23 10 9

Published in Great Britain by
Dorling Kindersley Limited.
A catalog record for this book is available
from the Library of Congress.
ISBN 978 1 4654 9409 2
Printed and bound in Malaysia.
A WORLD OF IDEAS:
SEE ALL THERE IS TO KNOW
www.dk.com

MIX
Paper from
responsible sources
FSC™ C018179

Every effort has been made to ensure that this
book is as up-to-date as possible at the time of
going to press. Some details, however, such as
telephone numbers, opening hours, prices,
gallery hanging arrangements and travel
information, are liable to change. The publishers
cannot accept responsibility for any
consequences arising from the use of this book,
nor for any material on third party websites, and
cannot guarantee that any website address in
this book will be a suitable source of travel
information. We value the views and suggestions
of our readers very highly. Please write to:
Publisher, DK Eyewitness Travel Guides, Dorling
Kindersley, 80 Strand, London, WC2R 0RL, UK,
or email: travelguides@dk.com

// CONTENTS

Left Lush rain forest bordering a
rocky beach and turquoise sea, Bali

Previous page An iconic yellow
taxi in downtown New York City

Front cover Walking in gorgeous
Alpine mountain scenery

// INTRODUCTION

Your bucket list is scrawled on the back of a well-thumbed postcard and pinned to the fridge door: see the Northern Lights dance across the Arctic Circle; celebrate the color-caked festival of Holi in India; spot penguins posturing off the shores of Patagonia. But where do you go from here or—rather—when?

It's the most-asked travel question—"so when's the best time to go?"—and it's often this uncertainty that stops us from seizing the day and clicking "book" on that trip of a lifetime. Besides, we've all had disappointing travel experiences, when the timing just wasn't right. We were promised secluded beaches and instead found the coastline congested with sun soakers. At other times, we would have preferred the hubbub of human activity, but the city streets were deserted. And don't get us started on the weather, when our dreams of endless sapphire skies were dashed by driving rain.

In *Where to Go When*, we've singled out the most unforgettable journeys, destinations, and festivals for every month of the year, so you know exactly when to set off on your next adventure. Not only that, but we've gathered mouth-watering photography that will stir your senses and transport you to faraway lands. We're certain you'll find new inspiration as you leaf through the pages. Perhaps you're looking for a getaway first thing in the new year, or you've earmarked September to October for a trip to distant shores. *Where to Go When* will provide you with a wealth of ideas—from electric events and festivals in Ethiopia and Albuquerque, through seductive scenery in the Maldives and Tuscany, to phenomenal wildlife encounters in Uganda and Borneo.

Travel adventures for every month, and in every corner of the earth, await between these pages. So pull up a chair, grab your bucket list and a pen, and let us show you where to go when.

Clockwise from top left
A reindeer in the depths of Lapland's winter; geisha chatting in Kyoto in early spring; the summer sun setting on St. Govan's Chapel, Pembrokeshire; a flowering tree in Mozambique in August

// JANUARY

A verdant shoreline
along the island of
Dhigurah, the Maldives

Above The dazzling Church of the Savior on Spilled Blood overlooking the Griboyedov Canal

Left Ascending the grand staircase of the Winter Palace; the snowy rooftops of the Smolny Cathedral and its convent

ST. PETERSBURG

Europe Russia
ST. PETERSBURG

WHY GO *January is in the thick of the Russian winter, when all those dreams of golden domes above snow-covered roofs, frozen rivers, hearty food and drink, and troikas (horse-drawn carriages) trotting along the icy streets come true.*

Not far beyond the borders with Finland and Estonia is St. Petersburg, a Russian jewel that glitters beside the Neva River. Founded three centuries ago by the larger-than-life, modernizing Tsar Peter the Great, St. Petersburg was conceived as, and remains today, Russia's "window on the west."

Peter created his new capital on a marshy site that had to be drained by the canals that now add so much to its beauty. St. Petersburg's lovely, sweeping waterways draw comparisons with the likes of Venice and Amsterdam, and the splendor of its broad, planned avenues, monumental Rococo and Classical buildings, and lovely parks certainly has a European orderliness and pomp—but all with an unmistakable Russian twist. The result is a visual grandeur that will take your breath away—most sharply around the stunning gold, mint green, and white Winter Palace, overlooking the broad Neva, and along the main artery, the Nevsky Prospekt.

The Winter Palace is today the centerpiece of the State Hermitage Museum, home to one of the world's great art collections and the showcase institution of a city that has always been a cultural capital. Russian ballet was born in St. Petersburg, and its streets are still stalked by the ghosts of Tchaikovsky, Dostoevsky, Rimsky-Korsakov, Nijinsky, and Pushkin, who all played out long passages of their often tragic lives here.

Spruced up for the 2018 FIFA World Cup, with dazzling creative spaces across the city, today St. Petersburg has an excitingly dynamic entertainment and nightlife scene, plus a good variety of eating and shopping options, making it one of eastern Europe's chicest cities.

When Else to Go
May Several public holidays mean parades galore. **June** During the month of White Nights, the city doesn't see the sunset, making for longer days to linger in the sunshine.

PLANNING YOUR TRIP **Getting there** St. Petersburg is served by direct flights from many European capitals. **Getting around** St. Petersburg's large, efficient metro is the best way to travel. There are also suburban trains, buses, trams, trolleybuses, and *marshrutky* (minibuses). **Weather** The city is under a blanket of snow in January, and temperatures drop further at night. **Average temperature** 14°F / −10°C.

LALIBELA

Africa Ethiopia
LALIBELA

WHY GO *Lalibela is affectionately called "Africa's Petra" thanks to its stunning rock-hewn churches. The town's unique mysticism is tangible in January when locals celebrate* Leddet *(Christmas) and* Timkat *(Epiphany).*

High in the wild and rugged Lasta Mountains, Lalibela ranks among the greatest religio-historical sites found on the African continent. The town's 11 medieval churches sit in carved rock recesses, their roofs at ground level, and give the impression that they have not changed for centuries; robed priests float among the dimly lit passages, and from hidden crypts and grottoes you can hear the sound of their chanting. The smell of incense pervades, while hermits, silent in the study of the scriptures, occupy tiny, rudely hewn holes. A steady trickle of pilgrims arrives, praying for health, wealth, and good fortune.

This ancient holy site is at its most alive at the start of the year. On January 7, the stream of pilgrims becomes a torrent as locals flock to celebrate *Leddet,* Ethiopian Christmas, among the awe-inspiring and truly unique churches. Then, on January 19, it's *Timkat,* the day of Jesus's baptism. Processions, chanting, singing, and dancing ring out from all corners, and the town is colored by the bright and beautiful textiles worn by participants. It feels as though you've traveled back in time. And in a way, you have. Biblical it seems and biblical it is; as the second country in the world to adopt Christianity (in around 350 CE), Ethiopia's connection to the religion is long and strong.

When Else to Go
October Fewer visitors, sunny skies, and a lush landscape make for pleasant exploration.

PLANNING YOUR TRIP **Getting there** International flights arrive into Addis Ababa, 400 miles (640 km) away, from where you can get a flight on to Lalibela. **Getting around** Internal flights are cheap if bought in Ethiopia. Car rental is available but expensive. **Weather** Lalibela's altitude keeps the heat down, with night temperatures dropping to single digits. **Average temperature** 66°F / 19°C.

Clockwise from top
An Orthodox priest
entering a rock passageway
connecting the rock-hewn
churches of Beta Medhane
Alem and Beta Maryam;
devotees approaching the
door of Beta Giyorgis, or
the Church of St. George;
a flock of pilgrims
surrounding the cross-
shaped Beta Giyorgis

North America US
JACKSON HOLE

WHY GO *Steep, deep powder and scenic beauty—this is the perfect time for all levels of skiers and snowboarders to hit the slopes of Jackson Hole.*

Left and below Skiers enjoying the deep powder on the slopes of Jackson Hole Mountain Resort

Among skiers, the mammoth mountain resort of Jackson Hole is legendary for its challenging terrain, including Corbet's Couloir, a narrow plunge only for the foolhardy or Olympic contender. For the rest of us mere mortals, there are all manner of groomed trails for effortless cruising and deep-powder snowfields that leave skiers and snowboarders desperate for more.

Situated in the heart of the dramatic Tetons, Jackson Hole Mountain Resort is in relative isolation in the northwestern corner of Wyoming. It is made up of two distinct mountains—Rendezvous and Apres Vous—which offer snow seekers plentiful and varied opportunities. Skiers and snowboarders enjoy clear and sunny weather in January, with the average snowfall 470 in (1,200 cm). One of the most ethereal moments occurs during a temperature inversion, when the valley is shrouded in fog but skiers above bask in blue skies; the sensation is of skiing off the mountain into the clouds.

When Else to Go
June Warmer weather makes for pleasant hiking around the mountains. **July–August** Classical music rings out across Jackson Hole as the Grand Teton Music Festival takes place across six weeks.

PLANNING YOUR TRIP **Getting there** The town of Jackson, Wyoming, has connecting flights from Chicago, Dallas, Salt Lake City, and Denver. **Getting around** There are regular shuttle buses between the town and ski resort. **Weather** Can be unpredictable, with blue skies or monumental snowfall. **Average temperature** 32°F / 0°C.

CLIMBING KILIMANJARO

There are various routes to the summit of this iconic mountain; here are our top picks.

1 **The Marangu Route** takes five days and is the most direct route to the summit. It passes through cacti fields and alpine meadows.

2 **The Machame Route**, the most popular trail, generally takes six days. Walkers are rewarded with an incredible array of views.

3 **The Lemosho Route** still feels relatively untouched and is regarded as the most scenic. It takes around seven to eight days.

4 **The Rongai Route** takes six or so days. It has less traffic than other routes, meaning you have a greater chance of seeing wildlife.

5 **The Northern Circuit Route** is the longest and most exciting route. Taking around nine days to complete, the 360°-views of the surrounding scenery are unrivaled.

TOP TIP

Remember that it takes time to acclimate to the change in altitude when climbing. A longer route generally allows for more rest stops and a chance to acclimate—plus you'll be rewarded with a greater variety of views.

KILIMANJARO

Africa Tanzania
KILIMANJARO

WHY GO *You'll avoid the long rains on the plains in January, making your ascent of kingly Kilimanjaro an even more memorable experience.*

The patchwork of savannahs dotted with giraffes, gazelles, or zebras that you see from your plane signals a gentle start to your Tanzanian adventure. But don't get too comfy— you're about to climb the highest mountain in Africa.

As your trek up Kilimanjaro progresses, the landscape alters constantly. First comes lush tropical forest resounding with the peeps and whistles of birdsong. Occasionally, through a gap in the trees, you glimpse a spectacular view of the plains below, a prelude of what's to come. Before long, the forest gives way to heathland. Giant groundsel and huge, spiny-looking lobelias colonize this corner, while birds and animals seem spookily absent. Then the heathland segues into desert, and altitude kicks in, declaring itself by

way of a thumping headache and seemingly unquenchable thirst. Soon tundra alters the environs again and you sense the end is in sight.

It's an early start at 1 a.m. on summit day. The tundra turns to dry, frozen scree, making the journey tough and treacherous. *"Poli, poli"*—"slowly, slowly"—comes the mantra of the guides, as a bitter wind blasts across the mountainside. At 4 a.m., however, temperatures begin to rise and, like a stage curtain lifting to reveal a beautiful backdrop, Africa's plains appear. At last, standing astride one of the Seven Summits of the world in the silvery light of morning, it's easy to understand the lure of this great African mountain.

When Else to Go
June–October Visit to see Tanzania's Great Wildebeest Migration.

Sleeping under the milky way at Barranco Camp, on Kilimanjaro

PLANNING YOUR TRIP **Getting there** Tanzania, East Africa, is served by Dar es Salaam, Kilimanjaro, and Zanzibar airports. **Getting around** Joining a tour is generally easier than tackling the climb yourself. **Weather** The altitude of the highlands tempers an otherwise tropical climate. **Average temperature** 82°F / 28°C.

PATAGONIA

South America
PATAGONIA

WHY GO *This seasonal journey takes you from Chile down to Argentina and reveals a landscape that is beautiful, desolate, and absolutely unforgettable.*

As dawn breaks on the Beagle Channel, the early morning light gradually illuminates the electric-blue ice of the floating glaciers surrounding your ship. The intense, wintry silence is broken by a thunderous crack as a huge chunk of ice detaches itself and falls into the ocean. This is southern Patagonia: a land of tremendous glaciers, dense native forest, and incredible wildlife.

A cruise through the Strait of Magellan, from Punta Arenas in Chile to Ushuaia in Argentina, slowly reveals astonishing sights. Weaving through a sinuous network of channels and islands, the boat affords you a taste of this extreme land, from the vivid greens and fauna of the national parks to the biting winds that howl against the tidewater glaciers. Zodiac and walking excursions provide opportunities to explore this fascinating land and its outstanding wildlife. Around 4,000 Magellanic penguins crowd together on the Tucker Islets, their little black-and-white figures an irresistible spectacle. From the lookout at Pia Fjord, you can see the Pia Glacier edging toward the sea, and, at the Tucker Islets, dolphins escort your ship into the bay. Looking out over Cape Horn and beyond, the sensation is one of remoteness.

When Else to Go
March Cruises are more affordable, and tourist numbers drop, too.
November–December Warm weather and an abundance of wildlife.

PLANNING YOUR TRIP Getting there Cruises run from September to March. International flights land at Santiago, Chile; from here, fly to Punta Arenas, the starting point of the cruise. **Getting around** Frequent port stops mean you can explore on foot. **Weather** Mild with some rain. **Average temperature** 57°F / 14°C.

PATAGONIA'S BEST NATIONAL PARKS

1 **Torres del Paine National Park** is in Chilean Patagonia and comprises mountains and lakes. The impressive Cordillera del Paine mountain range is the park's crowning glory.

2 **Tierra del Fuego National Park** is on the Argentine side of the island of Tierra del Fuego. The scenery here is vast, wild, and home to a huge number of animals and birdlife.

3 **Laguna San Rafael National Park** is on the Pacific coast of Chile. The park is famous for the breathtaking Northern Patagonian Ice Field, which stretches across the landscape.

4 **Queulat National Park**, in Chilean Patagonia, has snowcapped peaks and lush forests. The park is home to the staggering Queulat Glacier, which hangs dramatically over a cliffside.

5 **Los Glaciares National Park** is in the Santa Cruz Province of Argentinian Patagonia. The incredible Perito Moreno Glacier *(below)* is found in this epic hinterland.

"This is southern Patagonia: a land of tremendous glaciers, dense native forest, and incredible wildlife."

Clockwise from top Spectacular Salto Grande waterfall, Chile; penguins gathering in Patagonia; a ship sailing through Chile's icy waters

Idyllic sandy beaches and lush vegetation stretching along the island of Herathera, the Maldives

MALDIVES

Asia Indian Ocean
MALDIVES

WHY GO *The Maldives is famed for its exquisitely clear waters and sun-kissed beaches. In January, expect clear blue skies and little, if any, rain—ideal for unwinding in paradise.*

Surely the only way to describe this clutch of remote and tropical islands, each with its own coral reefs and shallow, turquoise lagoons, floating in the idyllic Indian Ocean, is "heaven on earth." Here, you'll find coconut palms and fruit trees swaying in the breeze and pristine white-sand beaches peppered with beautiful shells of all shapes and descriptions.

Time spent in the Maldives transports you far away from the stressful realities of modern life, and resorts are on hand to make you feel at home here in paradise, with a focus on rest and relaxation. Your body clock gets back into step with the simple rhythms of nature governed by the rising and setting of the sun; only primitive needs—eating and sleeping—exist and are easily appeased. The body is toned by surfing and swimming; the spirit is revived by basking in sunshine and watching the spectacular sunsets; and the mind is rested. If you're feeling particularly adventurous, join a local scuba-diving expedition and discover the islands' magical underwater gardens, home to an astounding wealth of marine life.

It's warm and humid at this time of year, with a cool sea breeze breaking the languorous nature of the heat. The dry season runs from December to March, and though a gentle northeast monsoon hits the islands, the skies stay clear blue and the water remains peaceful and calm.

When Else to Go
March–April Underwater visibility is good in spring, making this a great time to swim with whale sharks and, if you're lucky, manta rays.

PLANNING YOUR TRIP **Getting there** Most international flights arrive at Velana International Airport, on Hulhulé. SriLankan Airlines is the busiest carrier, with frequent flights. **Getting around** *Dhonis* (wooden boats) are a popular way of getting around, as are seaplanes. Malé and some larger islands offer taxis, but most islands are small enough to cover on foot. **Weather** January has warm days cooled by sea breezes. **Average temperature** 84°F / 29°C.

TROMSØ

Europe Norway
TROMSØ

WHY GO *Time and place are both key when it comes to seeing the Northern Lights, and January offers a great chance to check the bewitching* aurora borealis *off your bucket list.*

Magical and mystical, the *aurora borealis* dances over Tromsø's inky night sky in a shimmering spectacle of exquisite colors. The intense green, red, pink, and—on occasion—purple curtains of light are created from solar storms hurling charged particles into the earth's atmosphere but, to us, the *aurora borealis* evokes an extra-ordinary, ethereal illusion of infinity, a light show performed by the heavens. It's not surprising that the indigenous Sámi culture believes that the celestial aurora comprises lights shining from the souls of the dead, nor that the Vikings thought it was a bridge of fire built by the gods. Whatever the cause, you'll never forget the moment you witness the resplendent phenomena waltz against a cloak of stars.

Those searching for the *aurora* head far north to Tromsø, a city 217 miles (350 km) deep in the Arctic Circle, on the island of Tromsøya. Here in Tromsø and its surrounding wilderness of craggy, snowcapped peaks, the Northern Lights can be glimpsed from October to March, when the city sees 20 hours of daily darkness. In January, you have the best chance to enjoy cloudless skies, plus musical performances against the backdrop of the *aurora* as the city celebrates the Northern Lights Festival.

When Else to Go
February–March More clear skies to glimpse the Northern Lights.
May–July The ethereal midnight sun means endless days.

PLANNING YOUR TRIP **Getting there** Tromsø Airport is 3 miles (5 km) from the city center and receives flights from Norway's main cities. **Getting around** City buses provide reliable transportation. Car rental is a good option if venturing outside of Tromsø. **Weather** Snow is guaranteed, and wind chill makes the climate seem even colder. **Average temperature** 23°F / −5°C.

WINTER EXPERIENCES

Aurora chasers will find plenty to keep them busy in Tromsø and its surrounding Arctic landscape.

A wildlife fjord cruise is an amazing way to spot native animals, even in winter. Boats depart from Tromsø and passengers might see puffins, orcas, and even humpback whales.

Fjellheisen cable car ascends Mount Storsteinen, which has superb views of Tromsø and is a great spot to see the Northern Lights.

Arctic reindeer encounters include sleighing and feeding these native creatures. Such activities highlight the lives of the Sámi people.

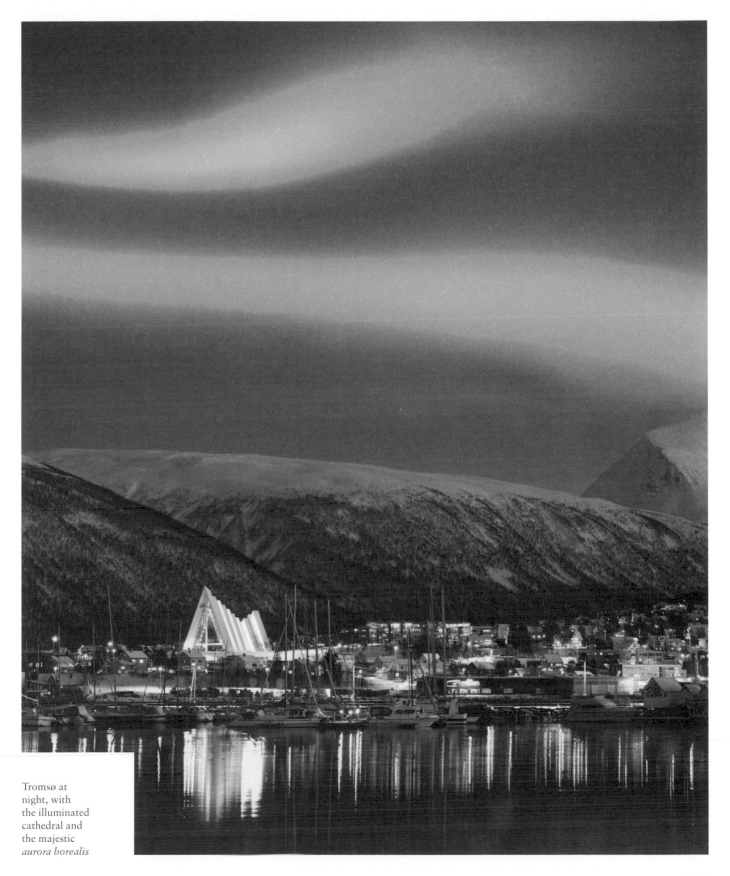

Tromsø at night, with the illuminated cathedral and the majestic *aurora borealis*

Sun setting over
Wat Arun and
the Chao Phraya
River, Bangkok

Walking along
Negril's Long
Bay Beach at
sunset, Jamaica

Asia Thailand
BANGKOK

WHY GO *January is relatively dry in Bangkok. Western and Chinese New Year both offer a sense of celebration.*

At first sight, Bangkok is an incomprehensible, sprawling megalopolis, home to more than eight million people and tuk-tuk–tangled traffic. Look further and Bangkok has an astonishing beauty and grace: in the morning, watch the humid mist lift from the Chao Phraya River, revealing the golden spiraling towers of the Grand Palace and surrounding temples glistening in the distance. Stop and you'll see the small details that imbue life here. Shopkeepers present food and incense offerings to little Buddha statues; street cooks toil behind sizzling stoves; and monks carefully prepare the city's temples for the day ahead.

Founded in 1782, Bangkok was destined to be even more exuberant than the old capital it replaced, Ayutthaya. A sense of the past can be experienced in Thonburi, where the narrow canals wind through an atmospheric maze of stilt houses, temples, and waterfront shops—a scene that hasn't changed for centuries. South of the city, the floating market at Damnoen Saduak is abuzz, and its floating shops and restaurants are perfect for roaming.

When Else to Go
April *Songkran*, the Thai New Year, is celebrated with water fights. **November** Bangkok's Wat Saket is draped in red cloth for Golden Mount Temple Fair festivities.

PLANNING YOUR TRIP **Getting there** Suvarnabhumi International Airport is around 45 minutes by taxi from the downtown areas. Some budget airlines use the Don Muang Airport. **Getting around** The Skytrain is the fastest way to get around, but it doesn't serve all areas, so combine it with boats, taxis, or tuk-tuks (agree on a price first). **Weather** Sunny and hot. **Average temperature** 90°F / 32°C.

JAMAICA

Caribbean
JAMAICA

WHY GO *Sultry and soulful, Jamaica is a heady mix of unique culture and cuisine, rich history, gorgeous beaches, and dramatic scenery. The highlights of this Caribbean country are best sampled during January's perfect, balmy temperatures.*

White-hot beaches dissolving into bathtub-warm waters; sparkling waterfalls tumbling through emerald forests; tree-covered mountains soaring to 7,200 ft (2,200 m)—Jamaica is a treasure trove of beautiful sights, but much more lies in store on this idyllic Caribbean island. Clamber up Dunn's River Falls, sail down the Martha Brae River on a bamboo raft, or seek out manatees in the swampy wetlands of the Black River Great Morass. Be sure to end the day at the Negril cliffs of West End, where you can catch a concert and watch the sun slide below a molten sky.

When Else to Go
July The sounds of Reggae Sumfest fill Montego Bay. Hotel rates are generally cheaper at this time of year, too.

PLANNING YOUR TRIP **Getting there** There are two international airports: Montego Bay (Sangster) and Kingston. **Getting around** Buses, taxis, and rental cars are the best way to explore. **Weather** Largely clear and balmy. **Average temperature** 79°F / 26°C.

COSTA RICA

Central America
COSTA RICA

WHY GO *With a bounty of parks and wildlife reserves that buzz with life at this time of year, Costa Rica is the perfect place to experience the diversity of the Central American tropics.*

Scarlet macaws screech overhead, howler monkeys swing in the dense forest canopy, and crocodiles loll along riverbanks. This is Costa Rica, a menagerie unlike any other. The abundance of colorful wildlife is a major thrill of any visit to this tiny Central American country, where 6 percent of the world's biodiversity makes its home. Cloaked in a thousand shades of green, the nation is a patchwork of national parks and wildlife reserves spanning 12 different ecosystems—all ready to be explored.

The mountaintop cloud forests of Monteverde, draped in ethereal mists, are a world apart from the tropical dry forest of the Pacific northwest, the mangroves of Terraba-Sierpe, or the lowland rain forests of Corcovado and Tortuguero—the latter a watery world laced with canals perfect for wildlife viewing. All along the coast, lush forests spill onto long swaths of sand where marine turtles deposit their precious eggs and paw prints betray the passing of a jaguar. Then there are the steaming volcanoes that stud the mountainous spine; dive into bubbling hot springs around passive Arenal, then peer into simmering craters from the summit of Poás. To the south, the hulking grandeur of the nonvolcanic Talamanca range soars, and craggy Cerro Chirripó, Costa Rica's highest mountain, tempts hikers to ascend through cloud forest and *páramo*—a high plateau—for all-around views from the summit.

Stitching the ecosystems together into a seamless journey is easy given the country's small size and excellent transportation facilities. Many travelers prefer adrenaline-charged pick-your-own adventures as a way to immerse themselves in nature: quad-biking excursions, exhilarating zipline rides through the forest canopy, surfing in the ocean, or whitewater rafting on the Pacuare or Reventazón Rivers—with a wealth of yoga retreats and lazy beaches providing laid-back alternatives. Whichever way you explore it, Costa Rica will inspire you.

When Else to Go
August–September Great whale-watching opportunities in the Southern Zone, as mothers nudge their infants to the surface near Bahía Ballena. **October** Límon Carnival inspires a party on the Caribbean side, with floats, music, and costumes aplenty.

PLANNING YOUR TRIP **Getting there** Costa Rica's capital, San José, has an international airport, as does the city of Liberia. **Getting around** All of the country can be reached by bus, but it's best to explore by car. **Weather** January is in the dry season, and it's hottest in the lowlands. **Average temperature** 75°F / 24°C.

WHERE TO SEE COSTA RICA'S WILDLIFE

Costa Rica's diverse range of climates fosters an astonishing array of animals.

1 **Humpback whales** gather in the country's southwestern waters in late winter and late summer to perform spectacular courtship rituals, breaching the water and singing to potential mates.

2 **Brown-throated three-toed sloths** are found across the lush Caribbean lowlands. Look up from the trails near Cahuita and you'll spot moss-tinged adult sloths easing through the branches.

3 **Morpho butterflies** flash along forest paths in the gardens of Monteverde. The iridescent wings of these butterflies shimmer electric-blue when in flight.

4 **Scarlet macaws** gather in raucous, colorful flocks along the Península de Osa. In January, take a zipline tour through the canopy in Parque Nacional Corcovado to spot breeding pairs.

5 **Olive ridley turtles** flood the Pacific coast in an event known as *arribada*, when thousands of females vie for space on the beach to nest. You'll see them on the shores of Guanacaste and Nicoya from July to December.

Clockwise from top
Corcovado National Park, Osa Peninsula; crossing a suspended bridge in Monteverde Cloud Forest; a red-eyed tree frog

// FEBRUARY

Gentoo penguins
battling the wind and
snow in Antarctica

AGRA

Asia India
AGRA

WHY GO *February's warm, dry weather is perfect for enjoying Agra's majestic Mughal architecture, including the monument of all monuments—the Taj Mahal.*

As you wander around the preserved tombs, palaces, and forts of Mughal India, you are transported back in time. The Mughals' best craftsmanship was reserved for funerary architecture, and the Taj Mahal is, arguably, the ultimate example. As familiar as this incredible monument may be, nothing compares to experiencing it in real life. The marble absorbs and transforms in the light—a rosy pink in the dawn, white and pristine in the noon sun, dusky and sensuous in the shadows of evening, and ethereal and ghostly in the moon's diffused beams.

An hour's drive away is Fatehpur Sikri, the elegant red-sandstone capital that Emperor Akbar built in 1585. Walking from immaculate courtyard to courtyard, you can almost hear Sufi music coming from a nearby shrine, played for the dancers performing on the giant chessboard floor. Peer through the windows into the shady palace suites and picture them filled with the laughter of the harem as women float through the rooms draped in a kaleidoscope of fine silks and muslins.

Descendents of the craftsman who created these timeless monuments today sell beautiful marble inlay bric-a-brac and fine embroidery in the bazaars of Agra. This remains a city bustling with true Indian energy.

When Else to Go
October–November Cool, dry climate after the monsoon season.

PLANNING YOUR TRIP **Getting there** Indira Gandhi International Airport is less than 6 miles (10 km) from Agra. **Getting around** Choose from auto rickshaws, *tongas* (horse-drawn carriages), cycle rickshaws, and taxis. **Weather** February days are pleasantly mild, and the rains haven't yet arrived. **Average temperature** 77°F / 25°C.

A boatman on the Yamuna River gliding past the Taj Mahal at dawn

HAVANA

Caribbean Cuba
HAVANA

WHY GO *February's sunny, dry days are great for exploring this historic city, while the cooler evenings are ideal for dancing the night away in a salsa club.*

Cuba's pulsating capital moves to an inescapable beat. Ever since the Tropicana exploded onto the scene, Havana's Afro-Latin music and dance have captured the world's imagination. It all took off in 1939 when a brilliant idea was conceived in a suburban villa with a vast, sprawling tropical garden: rig an open-air stage through this jungle setting and fill the walkways with hundreds of performers, in thrall to a loud Afro-Latin beat, costumed lavishly and choreographed lasciviously enough to waft any audience away into an exotic wonderland. The Tropicana, which came to typify the prerevolutionary decadence of Batista's Cuba, even survived the revolution. These days, February is the perfect time to visit. With very little rainfall—if any—you can spend a night in the balmy outdoors as the show continues on into the early hours.

Havana, too, like the Tropicana, is full of rhythmic sounds and throbs with music: thumping Reggaeton beats blare from car stereos, waves rhythmically pound the Malecón, and the sounds of salsa drift from the open windows of street-side bars. Poignancy pervades the city: patched-up dinosaurs of cars belch and clatter past crumbling mansions, barely lit by the streetlamps. Start in the Old Town, Habana Vieja, and admire the grand Baroque buildings of Catedral de San Cristóbal and Palacio de los Capitanes Generales, whose rich marbles and undulating lines hint at a refined and wealthy past. Next, head to Centro Habana to admire the Capitolio, one of the icons of the city. Inside, take a walk through the sumptuous "Hall of the Lost Steps" and listen for the eerie acoustics that give it its name. Later, visit Cuba's colonial past with a perfectly mixed mojito at the Hotel Inglaterra's rooftop bar and watch the stylish Cubans at play. Havana may be pushing on into the future—with a wealth of cool bars and stylish eateries now scattered across the city—but a haunting sense that Havana stopped in 1960 lingers on, making this one of the most fascinating cities on earth.

When Else to Go
July–August The Carnaval de la Habana is not to be missed. This weeklong celebration fills Havana's streets with sound and colorful parades.

PLANNING YOUR TRIP **Getting there** The main airport is José Martí, located 9 miles (15 km) southwest of Havana. **Getting around** The cheapest and easiest ways around Havana are taxis, coco-taxis (motorbike-powered two-seaters), bike rental, and on foot. **Weather** February is the driest, least humid month, with sunny days cooled by the northerly trade winds. **Average temperature** 72°F / 22°C.

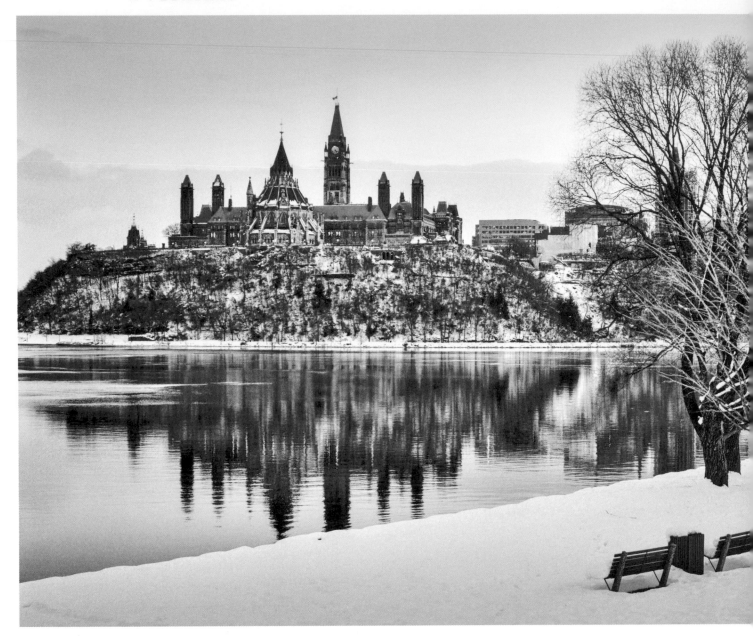

Above Ottawa's Parliament Buildings overlooking Ottawa River in the snow

Left The colorful Tunnel of Lanterns, erected in Confederation Park for Winterlude; an ice carver working on a sculpture during Winterlude

OTTAWA

North America Canada
OTTAWA

WHY GO *Winterlude lasts for two to three weeks in February, but most concerts, races, and activities take place on the weekends. Come for a short break to enjoy the festival and the city's highlights.*

Ottawa is blessed (or cursed) with some of the coldest winters of any national capital, which transform the city into a winter playground. The snow often starts to fall in November and hangs around until as late as April, meaning people have two choices: huddle indoors or make the best of it. Many Ottawans disregard the thermometer and spend the winter season enjoying all the sports, shopping, and museums that the Canadian capital has to offer. Strap on a pair of ice skates and join the locals gliding along the glassy ice surface of Ottawa's Rideau Canal, past elegant embassies and under arched bridges.

During Winterlude, Ottawa's parks resound with the buzz of chainsaws and the tap of chisels as artists create beautiful gleaming sculptures from ice and snow, and kids shriek on dogsled rides or have their flushed faces painted. When you eventually need to warm up, you'll find plenty of indoor activities across the city. Visit the antique steam locomotives at the Canada Science and Technology Museum or the dinosaur skeletons and other fossils at the Canadian Museum of Nature. Don't miss the bustling ByWard Market neighborhood, with its colorful street art, hip craft shops, and eateries. The ByWard Market Building on George Street is home to a food market; stop here to feast on Canadian specialities including cheese and maple-flavored chocolate.

As night falls, and the temperature drops even further, head to the warm, inviting lights of cafés and bars. On weekend nights during Winterlude, you can join music lovers wrapping their mittened hands around steaming cups of hot chocolate and huddling shoulder to shoulder to watch an eclectic array of bands. These outdoor concerts take place under a glittering canopy of city lights and twinkling stars.

When Else to Go
May Tiptoe through a million tulips blanketing Ottawa and revel in tulip mania at the Canadian Tulip Festival in mid-May.

PLANNING YOUR TRIP **Getting there** Ottawa is well served by international flights, and the airport is 20 minutes from the city center. There are also air, bus, and train links from other Canadian cities. **Getting around** Ottawa is easily explored on foot. The O-Train and buses serve the city center and outskirts. **Weather** In February, the skies are generally cloudy; snow and/or rain is likely. **Average temperature** 16°F / –9°C.

ZERMATT

Europe Switzerland
ZERMATT

WHY GO *The powder slopes around Zermatt are at their best in February—your snow-filled adventure awaits.*

In this quintessential Swiss village, picturesque chalets dot the hillsides and horse-drawn sleighs ply the main street, all under the watchful gaze of Switzerland's mighty Matterhorn mountain. The friendly atmosphere during the day turns positively festive after dark, as groups of friends wander toward a restaurant or club, stopping along the way to window shop at the elegant boutiques along the way.

When it's time to hit the slopes, you have many options. Nearly half of Europe's peaks reaching more than 13,125 ft (4,000 m) surround Zermatt, and each summit promises staggering vistas. Choosing a gentle, groomed piste is a great way to let your equipment think for itself so that you can admire the surroundings. If you're an enthusiast, why not participate in the incredible ski safari? It's made up of three connected peaks: the Rothorn, the Gornergrat, and Klein Matterhorn.

When Else to Go
July–August Enjoy culinary, music, and arts festivals, plus superb hiking opportunities.

PLANNING YOUR TRIP **Getting there** Zermatt is accessible by train from Switzerland's Zürich, Geneva, and Basel airports. **Getting around** The village is walkable (and car-free). **Weather** Sunny and snowy days. The mountain summits are very exposed. **Average temperature** 27°F / −3°C.

Climbing up to the starting point of the Marinelli Couloir, in the Swiss Alps

ANGKOR WAT

Asia Cambodia
ANGKOR WAT

WHY GO *February skies are brilliant blue and cloudless. Walking or cycling on the dry, shady forest paths around the temples is a delight.*

At dawn, as if on cue, the silence at Angkor Wat is suddenly broken by the piercing trill of cicadas. The first rays of the sun appear behind the darkened silhouette of the temple, slowly rising over the five lotus-bud-shaped towers and illuminating the long causeway. It is a magical moment in a mystical place that has witnessed each new day since the 12th century.

Aligned with the sun and the moon, Angkor Wat, with its towers, galleries, courtyards, and moat, is the biggest religious monument in the world. It is alive with vivid sculptures, and the morning light is perfect for looking at bas-reliefs of mythical battles that look more like ballets and scenes from Hindu epics. As you climb toward the central sanctuary, marvel at the detail of the many exquisitely carved *apsaras*, the celestial dancers, with their voluptuous figures, towering headdresses, and enigmatic smiles.

After such grandeur, head for smaller temples, like Ta Prohm. When you get to the temple, still covered in jungle, its collapsing galleries swathed in huge silk-cotton trees that pry apart the stones, it's like finding a lost city. Deeper in the forest lies an even older temple, Banteay Srei, a miniature, fairy-tale temple in red sandstone, covered with 10th-century carvings. At sunset, climb Phnom Bakheng, the temple mountain where, in the distance, you can see the five towers of Angkor Wat turn to gold in the fading light. If you are lucky, you'll witness the flight of the bats as they emerge from the nooks and crannies to feed, before everything slowly disappears into the shadows and darkness descends again.

When Else to Go
October The end of the rainy season is a quieter time to visit, but be prepared for torrential rain in the afternoons.

Above Sunrise over Angkor Wat, Cambodia

Right Carved figures outside the South Gate; the beautiful ruins of Ta Prohm temple, with a tree lodged in the masonry; a Buddhist monk

PLANNING YOUR TRIP Getting there Flights arrive at Siem Reap, 4 miles (6 km) from Angkor Wat. **Getting around** Hire a tuk-tuk with a guide who will take you around the temples for a fee, or rent a bicycle so you can see the sites at your own pace. **Weather** Dry, bright, tropical, and hot. **Average temperature** 81°F / 27°C.

Idyllic white-sand beach, bordered by palms and lapped by gentle waves, Mu Ko Ang Thong National Park

MU KO ANG THONG
NATIONAL PARK

Asia Thailand

MU KO ANG THONG NATIONAL PARK

WHY GO *You'll be treated to warm weather and calm seas in February, so whether you plan to snorkel or relax on a beach, your visit to this gorgeous national park will be unforgettable.*

The first approach to the 42 islands of Mu Ko Ang Thong National Park is always stunning. Rocky outcrops covered with deep green vegetation, interspersed with hidden coves and sublime sandy beaches, appear one by one from the glistening turquoise sea. Their strange shapes have inspired appropriately bizarre names such as Neck Island, Sleeping Cow, and Rhinoceros Island, which add to their mystical attractions.

The waters around the islands of Hin Nippon and Ko Wao offer some of the park's best snorkeling—the huge, brainlike corals found here are truly spectacular. Ko Wua Talab is a coconut-covered island with probably the most beautiful beach in the park.

But the true highlight of any tour is a visit to gorgeous Ko Mae Ko, where a mountain hike will lead you to a lookout over Thale Noi, a hidden turquoise saltwater lake. From here, you can see across the whole archipelago, as well as the two larger neighboring islands that sit outside the marine park, Ko Tao and Ko Pha Ngan. Explore the clear waters around Ko Tao, which boast some of the best marine life that Thailand has to offer. Or seek out one of the many island beaches where, protected by limestone cliffs, you'll find your own secluded hideaway.

When Else to Go
March–May This is the best time to spot huge whale sharks off Ko Tao.

PLANNING YOUR TRIP **Getting there** Flights arrive into Bangkok, from where you can catch a domestic flight to Ko Samui. **Getting around** To reach the marine park, take a boat tour or rent a local fishing boat. Ko Tao and Ko Pha Ngan can be reached by ferry. **Weather** Days are warm and dry. **Average temperature** 81°F / 27°C.

SPECTACULAR DIVING SPOTS

The clear waters and rich marine life in Mu Ko Ang Thong National Park offer superb opportunities for snorkeling and scuba diving. Discover coral reefs teeming with small fish and explore wonderful shallow caves. Here are some great places to get beneath the waves.

---

1 The beautiful corals at **Ko Wao** are home to angelfish and blue-spotted stingrays.

2 Vibrant sea fans and bushy corals make rocky **Hin Yippon** a great spot for underwater photography.

3 See dainty clown fish and huge barrel sponges in the caves at **Ko Yippon Lek**.

4 **Sail Rock** is the most reputed dive site in the Gulf of Thailand. Whale shark spottings are most likely in April.

5 The waters around the tiny island of **Ko Sam Sao** have some of the park's best coral reefs.

NORTH ISLAND

Oceania New Zealand
NORTH ISLAND

Right Steam drifting across
Champagne Pool at Wai-O-Tapu
Thermal Wonderland near
Rotorua, North Island

Below Fern leaves, a common
sight in New Zealand; a Māori
whakairo rākau (wood carving)

WHY GO *February falls in New Zealand's summer,
when you're likely to have the most reliable weather—
perfect for exploring the spectacular North Island.*

Imagine a land where everyone lives within easy reach of lush forest
trails, unspoiled beaches, gently rolling farmland, and sparkling rivers.
Where mountains are shrouded in legend and the surrounding islands are
subtropical idylls. New Zealand's North Island has all of this, coupled with
a sunny summer climate that is hard to resist. Renting a car or an RV to
tour the island will enable you to really experience all that is offered.

At its volcanic heart, vast lakes are cradled in ancient craters, and
towering volcano cones are powerful reminders of the landscape's turbulent
past. In this geothermal paradise, the land itself seems alive; geysers spout
plumes of boiling, mineral-rich water, steam drifts eerily across a lunar
landscape, and slurping cauldrons of bubbling mud plop lazily. These
natural phenomena are key to the ancient Māori culture that can still
be observed on the island. There's a real sense of openness here, in the
landscape and the friendliness of its people. The North Island will
astound you and fill your mind with countless picture-postcard scenes.

When Else to Go
September Wellington, the New Zealand's capital city, hosts its famous
two-week World of WearableArt festival, featuring spectactular garments.
Book tickets and accommodations well in advance.

PLANNING YOUR TRIP **Getting there** Most international flights
arrive in Auckland. **Getting around** Car and RV rental is available in cities,
major towns, and airports. **Weather** February is warm but changeable.
Average temperature 75–86°F / 24–30°C.

UGANDA

Africa
UGANDA

WHY GO *As the forest canopy thins out during Uganda's dry season, spotting gorillas on a trek becomes an exciting possibility.*

The atmosphere in the distinctly thick jungle of Bwindi Impenetrable National Park, located in one of earth's wildest regions, is so tense and charged that you can almost hear it crackle. This uncultivated rain forest is the habitat of some of Africa's last troops of mountain gorillas. It's as difficult to navigate as the park's name suggests, and finding a path through the thick and thorny primeval forest—on a fantasy expedition to find the elusive apes—is as off-script as it is unexpected. Shadows play tricks on you from under every branch as you climb steep verges and cross rivers.

The jungle, a rough-and-tumble, daylong drive west of Entebbe or Kampala, is a place of rain forest canopies, Tarzan vines, and buffers of rugged vegetation. While gorillas are the main draw, that's only the beginning. Keep an eye out for red-tailed monkeys, chimpanzees, jungle-residing elephants, and giant forest hogs.

The truth is you just have to get out there. Only then will you hear the wind whispering through all those leaves and realize there's a silverback before you.

When Else to Go
September–November Although the weather is generally misty and wet, this is the best time for bird-watching in the forest.

PLANNING YOUR TRIP **Getting there** Fly from Entebbe, Uganda's main airport, to the Kisoro airstrip, or drive from Entebbe or Kampala. **Getting around** The Bwindi park is best accessed as part of an overland tour or multiday safari. Purchase gorilla-trekking permits in advance. **Weather** Dry and hot. **Average temperature** 75°F / 24°C.

UGANDA'S BEST NATIONAL PARKS

1 **Queen Elizabeth National Park** has an unrivaled number of animal species, which includes elephants, hippos, buffalo, and the rare tree-climbing lion.

2 **Murchison Falls National Park**, in northwest Uganda, is renowned for its spectacular cascades, which sees the Nile River flushed through a narrow gorge.

3 **Lake Mburo National Park** is a wetland and savannah that can be seen by 4WD and boat. Expect to see zebras, impalas, and waterbucks, plus hippos and crocodiles.

4 **Kibale National Park** has an evergreen rain forest and is the best place to see Uganda's primates, including chimpanzees, and red colobus and red-tailed monkeys.

5 **Rwenzori Mountains National Park** is also known as the Mountains of the Moon. The majestic range is home to snow-capped peaks and Africa's third highest mountain, Mount Stanley.

TOP TIP

Travel to Uganda during the dry seasons (June–September and December–February) and you're likely to spot a variety of animals gathered around watering holes.

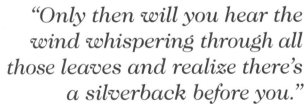

"Only then will you hear the wind whispering through all those leaves and realize there's a silverback before you."

Clockwise from top Silverback mountain gorillas in the dense jungle; sunrise and mist over Bwindi's forest; a group of trekkers looking for gorillas in the canopy

"A setting of incomparable beauty, Antarctica is one of the few untouched travel destinations left in the world."

ANTARCTICA

ANTARCTICA

WHY GO *The waters in this pristine paradise of icebergs and vast expanses of polar ice are navigable only during the summer (November–March). February is the best time to spot whales and see penguin chicks being cared for in their pebble nests.*

A setting of incomparable beauty, Antarctica is one of the few untouched travel destinations left in the world. Here, you'll spend your days cruising the frigid waves alongside humpbacks, orcas, and blue whales, picking a path between aquamarine icebergs the size of ships laden with lounging fur seals. As there are no piers or docks, you'll board rubber Zodiacs (inflatable boats) when it's time to set foot on the frozen continent, where you can take in the incredible icy vistas from close quarters and get acquainted with the wildlife. In the evenings, you'll use these boats to sail up close to giant icebergs, looming from the waves in the ghostly twilight of the Antarctic summer.

Best of all are the penguins, which are found in the thousands here in Antarctica—including six varieties peculiar to the south-polar region. The birds generally hatch their eggs around December, so by February the nesting sites are a rabble of noise and activity as the chicks prepare to fledge. You'll be kept at a safe distance from nesting penguins, but many birds seem oblivious and often waddle right up to investigate—resulting in unforgettable encounters.

When Else to Go

December–January Penguin chicks start hatching, and newborn seal pups appear. Temperatures are at their warmest, and there's up to 20 hours of sunlight.

Penguins walking on an iceberg, with the stunning blue ocean rolling below

PLANNING YOUR TRIP **Getting there** Prebooked cruises to Antarctica sail from Ushuaia, Argentina. Flights to Ushuaia depart from Buenos Aires, Argentina. **Getting around** Cruise ships enter the glacial bays, and Zodiacs are used to land on the ice. **Weather** Around 18 hours of sunlight; rain and snowfall are rare. **Average temperature** 34°F / 1°C.

MIAMI

North America US
MIAMI

WHY GO *Gorgeous swathes of sand, flamboyant Art Deco architecture, cutting-edge contemporary art, and a raucous nightlife—Miami is at its best in February, with mild, dry, sunny weather. The South Beach Food & Wine Festival adds extra cachet.*

You can laze on the city's seductive beaches, dance in the moonlight, or simply take in the sights and sounds of South Beach from a café on Ocean Drive—but there's much more to Miami, Florida's beating heart. Join a walking tour and admire the Art Deco hotels and condos, or paddle around the celebrity mansions of Biscayne Bay in a kayak. Sample the city's succulent stone crab claws and "Floribbean cuisine," a blend of Latin American and Caribbean flavors, before grabbing a cup of sweet Cuban coffee (*cafécito*) along Calle Ocho in Little Havana. Spend time perusing the boutiques of Coconut Grove and gallery hopping in Wynwood and the Design District. All of this—and don't forget the beaches.

When Else to Go
April–May Temperatures are heating up, but the beaches are rarely crowded. Miami Beach Pride week usually takes place in April, adding plenty of color, parades, and live music.

PLANNING YOUR TRIP **Getting there** Miami Airport is linked to the center by Metrobus, Metrorail, and Tri-Rail. **Getting around** Renting a car is the best option. South Beach and Downtown can be easily explored on foot. **Weather** Sunny and warm, with very little rainfall. **Average temperature** 75°F / 24°C.

Samba dancers
performing in the
Carnival parade,
Rio de Janeiro

South America Brazil
RIO DE JANEIRO

RIO DE JANEIRO

WHY GO *From the Friday before Ash Wednesday to the following Thursday, Rio de Janeiro shuts down for a week to host the world's greatest street party.*

Art Deco
buildings on
Ocean Drive
in South
Beach, Miami

Rio is a vast city with a mesmerizing setting, sandwiched between the balmy South Atlantic and jungle-smothered mountains. From its old Portuguese churches to its ramshackle favelas climbing the slopes at impossible angles, the city has some of the world's greatest sights. Perhaps most famous is the awe-inspiring statue of Christ the Redeemer, arms spread on iconic Sugarloaf Mountain. And let's not forget the beaches of Copacabana and Ipanema, and the Maracanã stadium, an icon to soccer fans.

Topping them all is Carnival, when Rio is at its most exuberant. Feathers and sequins glitter in the spotlights, massed drums boom, and huge loudspeaker-laden floats tremble as thousands of dancers twist and shake to a samba beat. The main event—the procession of Grupo Especial schools known as the

Desfile—takes place in the purpose-built Sambódromo, a long concrete structure that can accommodate 90,000 spectators. Each samba school competes on the basis of song, story, dress, dance, and rhythm.

There's more besides. You might stumble across an impromptu street party, day or night, with processions featuring booming samba and thousands of dressed-up revelers. Or you could visit a neighborhood samba school to learn how the dances and floats are put together. Then there are the wild Carnival balls and live shows—wherever you end up, it's time to join the party!

When Else to Go
December–January Reveillon (New Year's Eve) sees millions partying on Copacabana Beach.

PLANNING YOUR TRIP Getting there Rio Galeão Airport is connected to the city center by taxi and express bus. **Getting around** Explore the city on foot, or use the metro or official taxis (especially at night). **Weather** Sunny and humid. Brief thunderstorms and showers likely. **Average temperature** 86°F / 30°C.

// MARCH

Clouds circling the epic
mountains of Nepal
as the sun sets

BARSANA

Asia India
BARSANA

WHY GO *The Hindu festival of Holi sees revelers coat one another in colored powders in honor of spring. Barsana, in north India, is unique for its legendary Lathmar Holi hilarity.*

Holi—or the "Festival of Colors"—bursts onto the Indian calendar in an explosion of color and noise, as everyone takes to the streets with handfuls of *gulal* (colored powder) and reckless abandon. Nothing reflects the spirit of Holi better than the rainbow powders that symbolize the change from drab winter into bright spring. *Gulal* is either used dry and smeared onto people or mixed with water and splattered from water guns and balloons. On the night before Holi, large *hola* (bonfires) are lit, and an effigy of the demon Holika is burnt, signifying the triumph of good over evil. The mood is jubilant, but it is as dawn breaks the next day that the festival erupts.

The festival has long been presided over by Lord Krishna, whose roots in the state of Uttar Pradesh give the festivities an increased fervor in the village of Barsana. Here, Lathmar Holi follows a distinct tradition in the few days before the main Holi festival. Armed with sticks, the women make the men dress in women's clothing and dance while clouds of flame-red, turmeric-orange, and electric-yellow powder cover the streets in a technicolor smog. This is a typically Indian festival, pulsing with sensuality, joy, and life.

When Else to Go
October–November Diwali sees public spaces festooned with colored lights, homes lit by clay lamps, and various fireworks displays.

PLANNING YOUR TRIP **Getting there** Barsana is about 71 miles (115 km) southeast of Delhi, where most international flights land. **Getting around** To reach Barsana, rent a car from the airport. **Weather** March is sunny and very warm, with temperatures dropping at night. **Average temperature** 91°F / 35°C.

Right Throwing a cloud of colored powder over revelers; a Barsana woman laughing during Lathmar Holi celebrations

Below A crowd sitting and conversing during Barsana's color-filled festivities

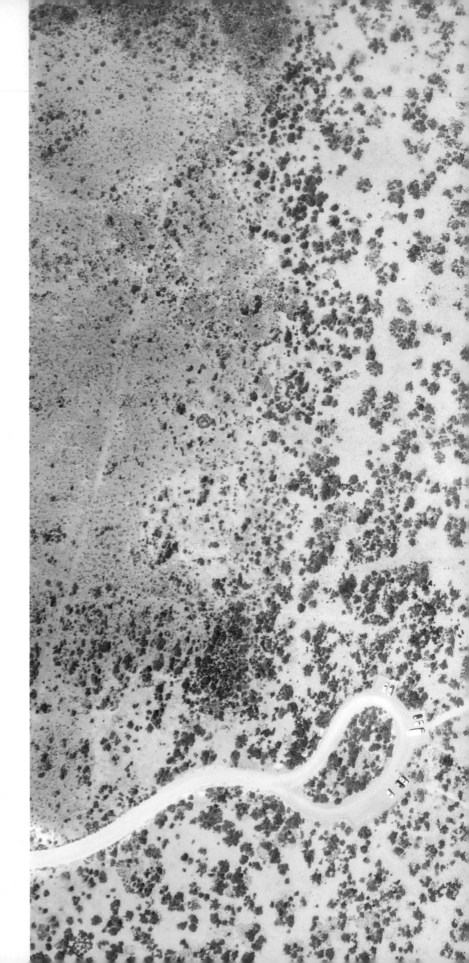

NINGALOO

Oceania Australia
NINGALOO

WHY GO *Whale sharks arrive around the time of March's coral bloom, making for an incredible snorkeling experience.*

Behind the blue curtain of the deep, Ningaloo's wonders beckon. For three months of the year, the warm waters off the coast of Western Australia encounters the mighty 50 ft (15 m) whale shark, looking to feast on plankton in the March coral blooms. The whale sharks are further joined by a legion of manta rays, clownfish, and starfish. Ningaloo Marine Park, stretching for 162 miles (260 km), teems with life and offers countless incredible underwater experiences. Dive at one of the world's top dive sites—Navy Pier—and watch all manner of marine life cruising the ocean floor.

When Else to Go
November This is a great time to see turtles nesting, manta rays, and humpback whales.

PLANNING YOUR TRIP **Getting there** Daily flights operate to Learmonth Airport from Exmouth, the nearest town. **Getting around** A 4WD vehicle is best. **Weather** Exmouth is warm year round with no wet season. **Average temperature** 68°F / 20°C.

Overlooking the aquamarine waters and rust-red landscape around Ningaloo Marine Park

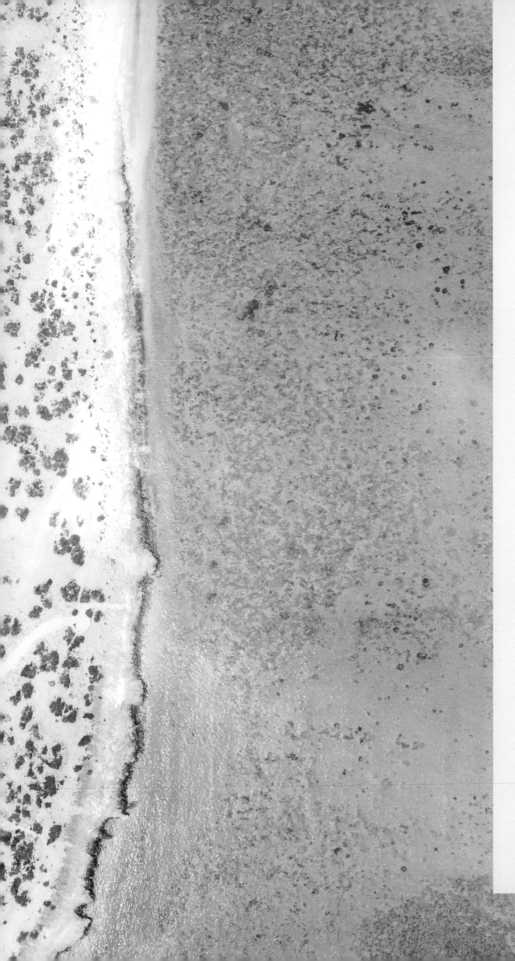

NINGALOO DIVING SPOTS

With a wealth of marine life and coral, the Ningaloo Reef is a diver's paradise. Here are three of the best sites.

Underneath **Exmouth Navy Pier** is an astonishing underwater world. Marvel at the giant groper *(above)* and the endless numbers of colorful reef fish.

Coral gardens and swim-through caves await in the waters around the two **Muiron Islands**. Look out for sea turtles *(above)*.

Dive sites in **Lighthouse Bay** feature limestone ledges and stunning coral formations. Whale sharks *(above)*, pelagic fish, and the rare frogfish are just some of the highlights.

HIMALAYAS

Asia Nepal
HIMALAYAS

WHY GO *The majestic Himalayas are home to nine of the world's highest mountains. Go trekking in March when it's mild and spectacular rhododendrons blanket the hillsides.*

Nepal is the crown of the Indian subcontinent, and the Himalayas, looming over the country with their snowcapped peaks, are an intrinsic part of any visit here. Of the country's mountains, Everest is, of course, the main draw, but the trek to the summit is hard work and only for the fit. There are also plenty of other trails which offer an equally thrilling experience. Passing through surprisingly lush valleys filled with wildflowers and stopping at Sherpa villages along the way, you will love all that this mountain kingdom has to offer.

When Else to Go
Mid-September–November Fall brings clear, sunny days and warm nights.

PLANNING YOUR TRIP **Getting there**
Flights arrive into Tribhuvan International Airport, not far from Kathmandu. Catch an onward flight to Lukla, the start of the trek. **Getting around** Hire a guide. Be sure you have the necessary permits. **Weather** Dry and mild but cold at higher altitudes (and at night). **Average temperature** 52°F / 11°C.

Khumbu Icefall, overlooking Everest Base Camp

Skiing through mountainside alpine forests in Whistler

WHISTLER

North America Canada
WHISTLER

WHY GO *It's all about the great outdoors in Whistler. Spring sees sunny days and powder aplenty, allowing for all manner of winter sports.*

This pretty resort village is cradled in one of the most scenic spots in western Canada. The Whistler and Blackcomb mountains dominate the landscape, with more than 200 ski runs, 16 alpine bowls, and three glaciers. Quiet trails through thick forests of fragrant pine and cedar beckon cross-country skiers, while the icy surface of the frozen Green Lake seems purpose-made for ice skating. And then there's heli-skiing, snowtubing, ice climbing, and so much more besides.

When you've had your fill of thrills, Whistler is a surprisingly cosmopolitan place to while away the evening. Enjoy an après-ski craft beer or cocktail at one of the many lounge bars and take in the spectacular scenery.

When Else to Go
December Plenty of Yuletide cheer, sleigh rides, and an annual film festival.

PLANNING YOUR TRIP Getting there
Flights arrive into Vancouver and a shuttle continues to Whistler. Car rental is also available. Getting around A free shuttle provides transportation to the ski lifts. Weather Snowy and mild, though cold on the mountain. Average temperature 36°F / 2°C.

Above Revelers dressed as devils carrying flaming torches through the city streets

Right A burning *falla* underneath an explosion of fireworks at the Fallas Festival

VALENCIA

Europe Spain
VALENCIA

WHY GO *Anarchy erupts on Valencia's streets during March's Fallas Festival, a raucous romp of giant puppets, fireworks displays, and fiery festivities.*

Pumping out clouds of gunpowder smoke, the multitude of fireworks explodes with such ferocity that the ground vibrates. The explosions increase in volume until, before you know it, the ruckus stops and the crowd bursts into spontaneous applause. Today's *mascletà*—a daytime fireworks display—is over, and tomorrow's will probably be even louder. This is the Fallas Festival, a boisterous burst of colorful fireworks, explosions, and processions in honor of St. Joseph, the patron saint of carpenters.

From March 15 to 19, more than 300 huge, elaborate papier-maché sculptures—the *fallas*—are set up in the city streets to be inspected and judged on their artistic merit. There is an air of unruly celebration that slowly builds to a crescendo of hysteria and anarchy. Revelers are sustained by creamy hot chocolate and sugar-dusted churros, while hard-core partygoers seek stronger, around-the-clock stimulation in the many bars of the buzzing Barrio del Carmen.

On the final night, the sculptures are packed with fireworks and set alight. As the flames greedily consume each work of art, the ecstatic onlookers pull back to avoid the heat, while firefighters nonchalantly hose down nearby buildings, occasionally flicking plumes of water over the spectators. Within minutes, each sculpture, which has typically taken six months to create, has been burned to the ground in a spectacular fiery climax of wanton destruction.

When Else to Go
July Feria de Julio is a monthlong extravaganza of parades, fireworks, and concerts.

PLANNING YOUR TRIP **Getting there** The city center is accessible from Valencia Airport by bus, metro, car, or taxi. **Getting around** The city center is best explored on foot. **Weather** Valencia is pleasantly sunny in March, though it does get cooler at night. **Average temperature** 64°F / 18°C.

After a day of revelry, dive into the best of the city's rich cultural heritage.

Gothic architecture Valencia's historic center is filled with a wealth of Gothic architecture. Don't miss La Lonja de la Seda, the Silk Exchange, with its soaring twisted columns and intricate vaulted ceiling *(above)*.

Street art The best of the city's street art is in Barrio del Carmen. Our favorite is Julieta XLF's colorful kawaii-inspired scenes along Calle de la Beneficencia.

Amazing museums World-class museums abound in the city. Essential viewing is the Museo Nacional de Cerámica, with its opulent alabaster facade.

Marvellous markets From street fairs to covered stalls, Valencia's markets can't be beat. Head to Art Nouveau Mercado Central *(below)* for foodie treats, then scour open-air Ruzafa and Rastro for vintage treasures.

SAN SEBASTIÁN

Europe Spain
SAN SEBASTIÁN

WHY GO *San Sebastián is the jewel in Spain's culinary crown, and March is a great time to quaff Basque cider and join locals on the* pintxos *trail.*

Lovers of the good things in life will feel at home in San Sebastián. One of the top culinary destinations not only in Spain but anywhere in the world, this seaside Basque city is rightly celebrated for its *pintxos* (Basque tapas), its seafood, and its wine, and gourmands of all stripes pack its backstreet tapas bars and multi-Michelin-starred restaurants. Gazing out over the Bay of Biscay with a glass of *txakoli* (sparkling wine) is an unbeatable way to pass an evening, as is the *txikiteo*—a crawl of the Parte Vieja's tapas bars, where you can sample classic dishes like salted cod, veal cheek, and pickled anchovies. These are the places to tap into the rhythm of local life, particularly in the evening, when locals flood out of workplaces and into the cobbled streets. Even better, this is cider season, and there are plenty of opportunities to sample this celebrated local tipple.

Beach lovers will also love San Sebastián. Playa de la Concha sweeps in a golden arc along the city's northern edge. Named for its shell-like shape, the beach is hugged by the mountains of Urgull and Igueldo, and its sheltered waters are ideal for a dip.

Sun setting over the picturesque Playa de la Concha, San Sebastián

Any trip to San Sebastián should end with a ride on the funicular to the slopes of mighty Monte Igeldo, where a terraced lookout point is a spectacular spot to watch the sun melt into the horizon.

When Else to Go
August Semana Grande sees street parties and fireworks displays.
September Boat races take place in Playa de la Concha.

PLANNING YOUR TRIP **Getting there** San Sebastián Airport is east of the city center, which can be reached by bus, car, or taxi. **Getting around** San Sebastián is well connected by a bus network and cycle lanes, with various car and bike rental outlets. **Weather** Mild with some showers. **Average temperature** 57°F / 14°C.

ON THE PINTXOS TRAIL

For many, San Sebastián is synonymous with one thing: food. *Pintxos* are the Basque take on tapas, eaten over a glass of something chilled in drinking holes in lively Parte Vieja (Old Quarter), often as part of a bar crawl. Here are some typical dishes to whet your appetite.

1 The most famous of all Basque *pintxos*, the *Gilda* is a simple skewer of olives, peppers, and anchovies—a must try for anyone on the trail.

2 *Rabas negras* is a striking take on classic calamari—fried rings of squid cooked in its own ink, lending it a deep black color.

3 Much beloved in neighboring Portugal, *bacalao* (salted cod) is also a long-time favorite; enjoy it skewered with peppers or deep-fried.

4 *Txuleta* is steak produced from mature, grass-fed beef. The Basques grill the beef to perfection. This is best enjoyed with a glass of red.

5 *Idiazabal* cheese is made from sheep's milk and is often served on small pieces of bread topped with quince and Iberico ham *(below)*.

CHICAGO

North America US
CHICAGO

WHY GO *Crowds flock to Chicago's streets the weekend before St. Patrick's Day (March 17) to follow joyous parades and admire the shamrock-green river at the biggest party outside of Ireland.*

Hundreds of green, white, and orange flags flap in the wind; Irish dancers pound out a rhythm on the asphalt, feet flying faster than the eye can follow; the bleating of bagpipes is punctuated with the happy shouts of children; and the piercing green river flows through the joyous revelry.

It's March in the Windy City and, for one rowdy midmonth weekend, Chicago transforms into a city of *craic*. Nearly a million local residents proudly claim their heritage as Irish thanks to mid-19th-century Irish immigrants who built this city. This explains the fervor with which St. Patrick's Day is celebrated here; this is, after all, the only US city to dye a river green in honor of Ireland's patron saint. Chicago hosts two grand parades on the Saturday and Sunday before the official holiday, drawing hundreds of thousands of Irish people—and Irish-for-a-day.

The Saturday parade is a family affair, while Sunday witnesses the more local South Side Irish St. Patrick's Day parade in the Beverly neighborhood, where increasingly boisterous partygoers inside the pubs can make for a more interesting show than the marching bands and floats rolling past.

Indeed, the parades are only part of the story. As early as Friday morning, revelers can already be found lining up outside the doors of the city's Irish bars, which swell with Guinness drinkers. Once the first parade is over, the partying truly begins, as parade spectators flood into bars, fiddlers provide a constant soundtrack, and the bacchanalian mood reaches fever pitch.

When Else to Go
June Time your visit with the Chicago Blues Festival and Chicago Pride Fest, plus early summer weather.

PLANNING YOUR TRIP **Getting there** Most international traffic arrives at O'Hare International Airport. **Getting around** Chicago's elevated railway is an easy way to get around the city, particularly during the St. Patrick's Day celebrations. **Weather** March is often overcast, rain is frequent, and snow is occasional. **Average temperature** 46°F / 8°C.

Chicago's river, dyed in honor of St. Patrick's Day, flowing between the city's iconic skyscrapers

PICTURE PERFECT

Marrakech's captivating colors and
golden light are a shutterbug's dream.
Here are some of the best spots.

1

As the sun sets, capture the frenetic energy
of the night market in **Jemaa el-Fna** from one
of the terraced cafés surrounding the square.

2

Ben Youssef Madrasa is a peaceful antidote
to the chaotic clammer of the medina.
Get there early to avoid the crowds.

3

For an explosion of color, head to the
Jardin Majorelle, where vibrant blooms
contrast with intense blue backdrops.

Koutoubia Mosque
overlooking the
buzzing evening
market in Jemaa
el-Fna square

MARRAKECH

Africa Morocco
MARRAKECH

WHY GO *The treasures that lie within the dusky pink medina walls of mystical Marrakech are best discovered in March, when temperatures are cooler and crowds are smaller.*

The spectacular Jemaa el-Fna, the main square in Marrakech, is the beating heart of the city, throbbing day and night with an extraordinary carnival of snake charmers, storytellers, acrobats, and musicians, all drawing enthralled crowds. In the evening, the square transforms into a giant open-air restaurant as hundreds of stalls sell traditional favorites, from delicious flame-grilled meats to *harira* (a thick lentil and chickpea soup) or—for those wishing to have a truly Moroccan experience—boiled sheep's head. Simply sit back on one of the many benches around the square and enjoy the sizzling, smoke-filled hustle and bustle of it all.

But there's more to this romantic old trading city. Head for the souks north of the square—a vast area of higgledy-piggledy cupboard-sized shops and stalls filling dozens of narrow alleyways. A delicious mix of heady aromas draws you further into the endless maze of lanes, where stalls are laden with bunches of fresh mint, jars of plump olives infused with lemon and garlic, mounds of succulent Medjool dates, and bright pyramids of spices. Intricately tooled leather, metalwork, brass lanterns, carpets, and jewelry are all here in abundance. Each area specializes in a particular item, so one street might be filled with colorful leather *babooshes* (slippers), the next with sparkling glazed pottery. Whether you are buying or not, it is a wholly entrancing experience.

When Else to Go
April–May Join locals for Ramadan as they break their fast in Jemaa el-Fna after sunset.
September–November Cooler temperatures make this a perfect time for sightseeing.

PLANNING YOUR TRIP **Getting there**
Flights arrive into Menara International Airport. Grab a taxi (agree on a price before leaving) or catch the No. 19 bus into the city. **Getting around** The city is best seen on foot or by bike, but taxis come in handy when it's particularly hot. **Weather** By March, the city is heating up, though temperatures drop at night. **Average temperature** 73°F / 23°C.

Pink-hued walls of Marrakech's ancient medina

YUCATÁN

Central America Mexico
YUCATÁN

WHY GO *The Descent of Kukulcán, down the northern staircase of the spectacular ancient Mayan El Castillo pyramid, can be seen from mid-February into April, but it is at its best on the spring equinox, on March 20 and 21.*

You sit with fellow onlookers watching the spectacle, awestruck. Brilliant sunlight picks out the tail of a giant serpent carved alongside the great north staircase of El Castillo, the pyramid at the heart of the ruined Mayan city of Chichén Itzá. As the day moves on, seven triangles of light form a zigzag on the steps and bring the serpent to life. This phenomenon—the Descent of Kukulcán—happens every year on the spring equinox. Aligned with the sun and stars with amazing precision, El Castillo was built around 800 CE. It has 365 steps around its four sides, one for each day of the year—effectively making it a huge clock.

When Else to Go

November The weather is dry and warm, but not sweltering, and tourists are yet to descend on the Mayan sights.

PLANNING YOUR TRIP **Getting there** Cancún Airport handles most international flights, Merida mostly domestic. **Getting around** First-class buses are a good way of getting around, but a car is useful if you want to explore more freely. **Weather** Tropical and hot, though cooler at night. **Average temperature** 88°F / 31°C.

Stunning El Castillo, sitting at the center of the Mayan city of Chichén Itzá

ANTIGUA

Central America Guatemala
ANTIGUA

WHY GO *Holy Week is a wonderful time to visit Antigua and experience the festivities. The air is filled with fragrances, and the streets are decorated with meticulous mosaic patterns.*

Lively strains of salsa and marimba music; the rhythmic pat, pat, pat of hands forming tortillas; the soft voices of Mayan ladies urging you to buy the bright woven *huipils* (blouses) that turn every market stall and courtyard into a vivid kaleidoscope—this is Antigua, Guatemala's former colonial capital, and one of the most beautiful cities in Latin America.

For one week in spring, the city takes on a whole new dimension, a sense of calm overlaying its usual lively buzz as residents pause to remember the most solemn of seasons in the Christian faith: Holy Week. The largely Catholic Guatemalans devoutly decorate the paving stones of their streets with intricate mosaics of bright blossoms and colored sawdust. Over these ephemeral carpets, robed men bear heavy statues of Christ in penance for their year's transgressions. The scene is beautiful and moving, an unselfconscious statement of faith encompassing sorrow as participants

remember the Via Dolorosa—the Way of Tears that Christ traveled to Calvary—and hope for a new beginning at Easter.

There's much more to explore in Guatemala. At the other end of the country, an untamed wilderness of jungle and swamps, stretching between Mexico and Belize, awaits. Temples atop Mayan pyramids break through the lush rain forest canopy—enigmas that have confounded archaeologists since the dense coverings of vines were first torn away to reveal their stones. Once a thriving city, Tikal was abandoned a millennium ago and is remarkable for its eerie desolation. Ponder its mysteries as you wander its winding paths, greeted by the cries of tropical birds and howler monkeys in the branches overhead.

When Else to Go
December The midmonth Palo Volador celebrates the Feast of St. Tomas, with bungee-like acrobats.

Right Processing alongside mosaics made from colored sawdust on Good Friday

Below A young boy swinging burning incense before a religious float

PLANNING YOUR TRIP **Getting there** Antigua lies 16 miles (26 km) from Guatemala City, where international flights arrive at La Aurora Airport. Buses and taxis connect to Antigua. **Getting around** For Tikal, frequent flights connect Guatemala City to Flores. Transfers are included in most tours or arranged on arrival. **Weather** This is Guatemala's dry season. **Average temperature** 72°F / 22°C.

// APRIL

The picture-postcard
village of Positano
clinging to the hills of
the Amalfi Coast

BERGEN

Europe Norway
FJORD CRUISE

WHY GO *Experience two seasons in one amazing voyage as you sail from Bergen, where spring is in full bloom, to Kirkenes, deep in the Arctic North.*

Norway's dramatic coastline is one of the world's natural wonders. Forested mountains stand with their feet in pristine fjords, their snowy peaks raked with cloud as waterfalls plunge into deep channels of icy water below. Nestled among them, wooden houses are painted in shades of mustard and cinnamon, briny fishing boats line pretty harbor fronts, and, in the cities, ancient history sits alongside the familiar hum of 21st-century life.

Every day of the year, a Hurtigruten (Coastal Voyage) ship leaves Bergen and heads north for Kirkenes, way above the Arctic Circle. The 12-day round trip takes in 34 ports, berthing in the craggy-peaked Lofoten Islands, the Arctic city of Tromsø, and Honningsvåg, home to the fascinating North Cape Museum. The hop-on hop-off service means you can jump ashore and embark on city tours, venture into glacier country, hike steep mountain passes, and encounter the Sámi way of life. This trip is truly a unique voyage of discovery.

When Else to Go
May Sleepy Bergen springs to life during Bergen International Festival, with music, ballet, theater, dance, and performing arts.

PLANNING YOUR TRIP **Getting there** Prebooked cruises sail from Bergen, served by Bergen Airport, Flesland. **Getting around** Bergen Light Rail links the airport to the city. **Weather** Sunshine, rain, and snow above the Arctic Circle. **Average temperature** 43°F / 6°C.

Clockwise from top left
Norwegian flag blowing in
the arctic wind aboard a
Norwegian cruise ship;
puffin perching on a rock
in Runde; the picturesque
town of Hamnøy in the
Lofoten archipelago

PETRA

Asia Jordan
PETRA

WHY GO *Petra's rock-hewn facades seem almost otherworldly as they reflect the swirls of color that pattern the surrounding hillsides. April promises cool temperatures and an abundance of wild blooms—the perfect backdrop to this "rose-red city."*

The ancient Nabataean city of Petra surpasses all expectations—to call it dramatic is an understatement. This spectacular city is truly one of the world's most atmospheric ancient sites.

Leaving behind a scorched and bleak stony landscape, you enter a narrow canyon known as the Siq, squeezed between vertical rock walls that are in places so narrow you can barely see the sky. This is the secretive entrance to a city that remained hidden to the outside world for more than half a millennium. Advancing along the Siq, the sense of anticipation grows, until you round the final bend and come face-to-face with the famous rose-pink facade of the Treasury, chiseled out of the solid rock wall. To the right, the canyon widens, its glowing veined walls sculpted with facades of columns, pediments, and ornate doorways. A little farther on stands a theater carved deep into the hillside, and beyond, a sandy-floored main street. If that was it, it would be staggering enough, but it's not. From here, you clamber up rocky staircases and passageways to yet more tombs and monuments, to the ruins of a Crusader castle, and to a great altar known as the High Place of Sacrifice, with fantastic views of the mountains and desert beyond. Petra is far more than just an archaeological site; it's a breathtaking adventure into the past.

When Else to Go

October Enjoy crisp days, cool nights, and splashes of fall color along Petra's watercourses.

PLANNING YOUR TRIP **Getting there** Jordan's capital, Amman, is served by Queen Alia International Airport. There are regular bus connections to Petra from Amman. **Getting around** Explore the site on foot or by calèche (horse-drawn carriage). **Weather** Mild and pleasant. **Average temperature** 71°F / 22°C.

UNMISSABLE SIGHTS

This spectacular Nabatean city is home to an overwhelming array of ancient wonders. Here are a few highlights.

Built into the rose-pink rock face in the 1st century BCE, the colonnaded facade of the **Treasury** is easily one of the most incredible sights in the Middle East.

A mesmerizing sight, the **Monastery** is second only to the Treasury in impact. The path to the site is carved into the mountains.

The **High Place of Sacrifice** is the best preserved of Petra's sacrificial sites. The altar at the summit is marked by two stone obelisks.

The utterly
breathtaking
Treasury, lit
by candlelight

"A golden sunlight makes everything shimmer, from tomb mosaics to vivid lapis-blue tiled cupolas."

Left Ornate mosaics adorning Samarkand's opulent Registan

Above Highly decorative ceiling in Samarkand's Shah-i-Zinda necropolis; an Uzbek man

SAMARKAND

Asia Uzbekistan
SAMARKAND

WHY GO *With its distinctive blue-tiled mosques, mausoleums, and madrassahs, Samarkand is a glittering gem on the Silk Road. April is the perfect month to visit this scintillating city, before the extreme summer heat and sandstorms set in.*

One of the most alluring of the ancient Silk Road trading stops, Samarkand luxuriates in a golden sunlight that makes everything shimmer, from tomb mosaics and vivid lapis-blue tiled cupolas, to the gold and silver threads that run the lengths of brightly colored fabric, silk rugs, and scarves piled high in the central bazaar. Here, the air is filled with the aromas of spices and *shashlik* (mutton kebabs) sizzling over hot, glowing charcoals.

Your first port of call here is the Registan—a vast square, framed on three sides by a trio of 15th- to 17th-century *madrassahs* (religious colleges). And it won't disappoint. Adorned with

delicate patterns and intricate floral, calligraphic, and geometric motifs in dazzling blues, greens, and golds, the scale and beauty of these buildings is breathtaking. But beyond the imposing minarets, colorful bazaars, and tranquil Islamic gardens lies another side to this ancient city. Soviet-style frescoes depict scenes of the Russian Revolution, crumbling Brutalist monuments pay homage to science and progress, and vodka is the tipple of choice —a hangover from Uzbekistan's Soviet past.

Samarkand is also an excellent base from which to explore. Drink green tea with the locals in nearby Bukhara, travel west along the Silk Road to Khiva, the

last outpost before the desert, or head south to trek the high ground of the picturesque Aman Kutan Mountains.

When Else to Go
October The temperature is pleasant and fall light illuminates the blue-glazed tiles of the city's buildings.

PLANNING YOUR TRIP
Getting there International flights arrive in Samarkand International Airport. High-speed rail links run from the capital, Tashkent. **Getting around** Buses are cheaper and more frequent than trains. **Weather** Sunny; rain is unusual. **Average temperature** 72°F / 22°C.

BOLLENSTREEK

Europe The Netherlands
BOLLENSTREEK

WHY GO *Late springtime in the Bollenstreek, the Netherlands' "Garden of Eden," is bursting and beautiful with the world's greatest flower spectacle.*

The moment you arrive in the Bollenstreek—a bulb-growing district famous for its vast fields of petal-perfect tulips, plus freesias, hyacinths, and daffodils—you'll understand why the Netherlands is the world's greatest bloom exporter. Beginning in January, the flowering season peaks in late spring with the arrival of late-blooming lilies and—the show stealer—fields covered by millions of tulips erupting in a rainbow of colors.

Most tulip tours of the region start in the charismatic city of Haarlem, the northernmost point of the Dutch flower empire. From here, the Bollenstreek stretches south for 25 miles (40 km), providing plenty of opportunity for you to soak up the perfumes and natural theater of springtime. For many, the undoubted highlight of the region is the Keukenhof, the celebrated flower garden of Lisse, which opened in 1949 and has some 10 miles (17 km) of pathways carpeted with row upon row of flower beds.

When Else to Go
February–March Crocuses and snowdrops are in full bloom, hailing the end of winter.

PLANNING YOUR TRIP **Getting there** Haarlem is served by Schiphol Airport. There are regular trains from Amsterdam. **Getting around** Rent a car or a bike and cycle between fields; everything is well signposted. **Weather** Sunshine is common, as are light showers. **Average temperature** 55°F / 13°C.

Left Row upon row of flowering tulips in the Bollenstreek

Below The charming waterside city of Haarlem, the starting point of trips to the Bollenstreek

KYOTO

Asia Japan
KYOTO

WHY GO *Kyoto comes alive in spring as cherry blossoms burst into bloom, creating a magical backdrop to this enchanting city. The custom of blossom-viewing—or* hanami—*is unmissable.*

Ancient Kyoto is the yin to modern Tokyo's yang, a city where elegance and philosophy permeate every aspect of daily life. Home to an impressive 17 UNESCO World Heritage Sites—13 Buddhist temples, three Shinto shrines, and the romantic Nijo Castle—Kyoto is, unarguably, the bastion of Japan's rich cultural landscape.

Springtime is awaited in Japan with keen anticipation; the meteorological agency even monitors the so-called "cherry blossom front," allowing the public to follow the flowering trees during the *sakura* (cherry blossom) season. In Kyoto, parks, temples, and public spaces are dusted with delicate pink and white blossoms, and the cultural events held throughout *hanami* are unparalleled. This is the perfect time to join the many who stroll along the Philosopher's Path—a pleasant canal-side trail lined by cherry trees that winds its way through Kyoto's Higashiyama district from Kiyomizu-dera Temple to Ginkaku-ji (the Silver Pavilion).

Beyond the blooms, Kyoto is known for its association with geisha (or *geiko* in the local dialect), the "arts person" who makes her home in one of Kyoto's *hanamachi* (flower towns). The geisha stage special cherry dances throughout the month of April, the most famous of which is the Miyako Odori, or "capital city dance," so named because Kyoto was once the imperial capital of Japan. The revered geisha and *maiko* (geisha in training) of the Gion Kobu perform their captivating art with grace and skill.

When Else to Go
November Enjoy blazing fall colors during the *koyo* (fall leaf viewing) season.

PLANNING YOUR TRIP
Getting there Kyoto is served by Kansai International Airport and is also around 2½ hours from Tokyo by bullet train. **Getting around** The city has a small subway system and bus network. **Weather** Sunny and mild. **Average temperature** 68°F / 20°C.

Right Traditional Japanese kimono textile; the striking Fushimi Inari Taisha at the base of Mount Inari

Below Sunset at Kiyomizu-dera Temple during the *sakura* season

IGUAÇU FALLS

South America Brazil
IGUAÇU FALLS

WHY GO *A thunderous display of the power of nature, the Iguaçu Falls are at their most dramatic in April, when they are swollen with summer rainfall.*

No waterfall on earth can match Iguaçu's combination of towering heights, soul-churning flow, and pristine rain forest setting. The falls straddle the border between southern Brazil and northern Argentina, where the powerful but slow-moving Iguaçu River splits and tumbles over a 2-mile- (3-km-) wide precipice, hurtling into the swirling waters of the cavernous gorge below with a deafening roar. Here, hundreds of perfect rainbows form in mist that hovers above the frothing water.

Experience the falls from a boat at the bottom of the cascade or on foot, from distant vantage points with long, sweeping vistas and on viewing platforms, where the falls' cool spray will soak you in a matter of seconds.

When Else to Go
August–September Water levels drop, revealing hidden rock formations behind the falls.

PLANNING YOUR TRIP Getting there The nearest city, Foz do Iguaçu, is a two-hour flight from Rio de Janeiro and São Paulo. **Getting around** Buses, taxis, and tourist vans ferry visitors around. **Weather** Clear and dry. **Average temperature** 64°F / 18°C.

Mist and spray rising from the pools of churning water at the magnificent Iguaçu Falls

Istanbul's iconic
Blue Mosque, one
of the most majestic
mosques in Turkey

ISTANBUL

Asia/Europe Turkey
ISTANBUL

WHY GO *Spring brings new energy to Istanbul. Before crowds arrive en masse and summer heat sets in, April is the perfect time to discover all that this cosmopolitan city has to offer.*

Istanbul, with its beautiful spiky skyline of delicate minarets and onion domes, is a city adorned with fantastic palaces decorated with riches gained in conquest. The city's roots as an ancient trading post are evident in the Grand Bazaar, with its covered passageways and glittering stalls. Here, you can lose yourself for hours.

A short stroll downhill brings you to the waters of the Golden Horn, spanned by the Galata Bridge that links the old city with the new. The main street, Istiklal Caddesi, and its network of tiny lanes are a cluster of boutiques, cafés, restaurants, bars, and clubs. It's here that you'll find creamy *tarama*, the best food in town, plus mussels stuffed with rice and spices, the obligatory kebab, and, of course, all manner of mouthwatering meze.

As a former capital of two major empires—the ancient Byzantine and the Ottoman Turkish—Istanbul is rich with imperial history, and the architecture that goes with it. The promontory of land known today as Sultanahmet was developed under centuries of emperors and sultans— its great walls enclosed long-since vanished palaces and some of the world's earliest Christian religious establishments. Today, among the many archaeological treasures, you can explore the magnificent Topkapı Palace, the Blue Mosque, and the remnants of the great hippodrome that was used for chariot races.

When Else to Go
October Istanbul's parks and gardens are ablaze with fall colors.

PLANNING YOUR TRIP Getting there Istanbul is served by Atatürk and Sabiha Gokcen international airports, with bus connections to Taksim Square. **Getting around** Most sights are within walking distance from one another, but there is also a large network of tram and metro lines and plenty of taxis. **Weather** Days are clear and mild. **Average temperature** 61°F / 16°C.

Istanbul loves a party. From May to September, the city comes alive with all manner of exciting summer festivals, but April features an impressive lineup with a much more local feel.

Tulip Festival Turkey's national flower is the tulip *(above)*. Every April, millions of bulbs bloom across the city. Roadside verges are a riot of color, but the flowers are best viewed in parks such as Emirgan and Gülhane.

Sokak Festivali Live music, entertainment, sports, and street food converge during this three-day street festival. Expect performances from the most popular musicians in the city and an eclectic mix of genres, from Balkan beats to funk, from soul reggae to electronica.

International Istanbul Film Festival Film buffs descend on Istanbul at the beginning of April. Since its inception in 1982, this festival *(below)* has screened more than 3,000 films from 76 countries. Most showings are held in theaters around Istiklal Caddesi.

Süleymaniye Mosque
overlooking Istanbul's
energetic harbor

South America Ecuador
GALÁPAGOS ISLANDS

WHY GO *The Galápagos offer the most incredible eye-to-eye encounters with wildlife. In April, the islands' air and sea temperatures are perfect for enjoying a dip.*

This volcanic archipelago is home to a menagerie of exotic creatures. The islands, which owe their unique quality to their isolation, were set aside as a national park in 1959, and visits here are regulated so as to protect the natural residents. A licensed guide accompanies each cruise boat to enforce park rules and educate tourists on the ecology.

Join a boat excursion and watch as manta rays glide under your vessel and bottlenose dolphins break the water's surface beside you. Dive in to join them, or the hammerhead sharks off Bartolomé Island, or sea lions in the waters around San Cristóbal Island. You can even snorkel with penguins off Fernandina. Go ashore to see the islands' namesake, the giant tortoise (*Galápago* is Spanish for tortoise), heaving its 610 lb (275 kg) weight up the beach.

Everywhere you turn, the islands' residents dance, dart, and dive—this is Eden for wildlife.

When Else to Go
June–August Blue-footed boobies perform their distinctive mating rituals.

PLANNING YOUR TRIP **Getting there** International flights arrive into Quito and Guayaquil, Ecuador. From there, catch a flight to Santa Cruz. **Getting around** Small ships and charter boats offer organized outings. **Weather** Pleasantly warm with some rain. **Average temperature** 81°F / 27°C.

Two Galápagos sea lions playing in a cove off San Cristóbal Island

PERHENTIAN
ISLANDS

Asia Malaysia
PERHENTIAN ISLANDS

WHY GO *With warm weather and stunning scenery, the Perhentians are perfect for a relaxing spring break.*

Welcome to the world of rain forests and coral reefs—two extraordinarily diverse natural habitats. The Perhentians comprise two main islands in the South China Sea, Perhentian Besar and Perhentian Kecil, with a peppering of smaller islands nearby. Lush rain forests are protected here by unending sandy beaches, lined with swaying palms.

Quite simply, this is paradise, one where you can spend hours watching nesting turtles, scuba diving above colorful carpets of coral and mesmerizing fish, partying on the sandy beaches until sunrise, or lying swinging in a hammock. These islands have it all, and, for a while at least, you can forget the world you left behind.

When Else to Go
May–July Experience peak turtle-nesting season on the islands.

Clear blue waters and bobbing boats off the shore of one of the delightful Perhentian Islands

PLANNING YOUR TRIP Getting there The nearest international airport is in Kuala Lumpur. Fly on to Kota Bharu or Kuala Terengganu and catch a bus to Kuala Besut—boats run to the Perhentians from here. **Getting around** A water taxi allows you to island-hop. **Weather** Expect sunny weather. **Average temperature** 88°F / 31°C.

ATHENS

Europe Greece
ATHENS

WHY GO *Dynamic and diverse, crumbling structures and contemporary sights live side by side in Athens. If this heady mix isn't enough, the Greeks embrace Easter with great fervor at this time of year.*

Greece's capital is nothing short of captivating. The historic center is an open museum, with a treasure trove of ruins and Byzantine churches sitting alongside apartment buildings and office blocks. Atop the imposing Acropolis is the majestic Parthenon—the symbol of the city. This titanic temple watches over the likes of the Ancient Agora, the Theatre of Dionysus, and the Sanctuary of Zeus, plus the Greek people milling about in the cobbled streets, as they did thousands of years ago. Today, though, the view also takes in striking street art, myriad bookshops, and cute cafés around every corner.

If you're in Athens at Easter *(Pascha)*, you're in for an extra treat. Holy Week begins on the Monday before Easter with a strict fast, and houses traditionally get their yearly whitewash. On Good Friday, church bells toll eerily all day; at around 8 p.m., candlelit processions wind slowly through the streets. At midnight on Saturday, locals meet outside churches with candles and watch fireworks. Celebrations culminate on Easter Sunday, with music resounding through the streets and the aroma of lamb from rooftop rotisseries permeating the air.

When Else to Go
August Ancient sites stay open for the full moon. **September** Athens Classic Marathon is based on the original route from Greek legend.

PLANNING YOUR TRIP **Getting there** Athens International Airport is about 45 minutes by taxi from the center. There's also a metro link, which takes 40 minutes. **Getting around** Sights are closely packed and easily walkable, though there are also buses and a useful metro system. **Weather** Sunny and pleasant. **Average temperature** 68°F / 20°C.

Above The Parthenon atop the Acropolis, overlooking the city rooftops

Right Freshly baked *simit*; the crumbling columns of the Parthenon; *Believe in Dreams* by Wild Drawing

Looking out over picture-postcard Positano from a shaded cliffside terrace

LOCAL FLAVORS

Indulgence is intrinsic to Italy, and the Amalfi Coast produces the country's best lemons and seafood.

1

Delizie al Limone are sponge cakes filled with lemon cream and sealed with a zesty glaze. Their name translates as "lemon delights."

2

Fresh seafood appears in various dishes, such as local favorite *polipetti affogati*— octopus "drowned" in tomatoes and wine.

3

Limoncello is a zingy lemon-based liquor, best enjoyed in a frosted glass paired with a sea view. The perfect end to a day of driving.

AMALFI COAST

Europe Italy
AMALFI COAST

WHY GO *A drive along the Amalfi Coast is best enjoyed in April, when villages shake off their winter slumber, sun-warmed lemons hang plump and heavy, and the scent of citrus blossoms lingers.*

The scenery gradually unfolds before you: towering cliffs plunge into the sea, azure waters pan out to the horizon, and villages cling to the craggy mountainside. Leaving behind gritty Naples and the ancient ruins of Pompeii and Herculaneum, your journey begins in earnest, wriggling along the Sorrento Peninsular, a cliff-edged promontory of sheer rugged beauty. Sorrento, the gateway to the Amalfi Coast, sits amid terraced lemon groves that, come April, are thick with fruit. The road then sweeps across the headland before gliding up the underbelly of the peninsular and its scattering of sandy coves, signaling your arrival at Positano. The Amalfi Coast's fashionable darling is an unmissable stop: a dramatic cascade of peach, cream, and blush buildings housing boutiques and eateries, tumbling to meet a crescent bay. From Positano, the road continues, its folds hitching up the whitewashed beauty of Praiano and scenic Amalfi. Yet it's the final stretch of road, from Amalfi to Salerno, that holds the most stunning scenery. Here, dramatic gorges and emerald caves pass by as the road climbs heavenward to the garden-draped terraces and poised cliffside villas of Ravello. It's clear you've saved the best for last.

When Else to Go
September Summer lingers, keeping things warm, and most of the crowds have returned home, leaving the roads and towns much quieter.

PLANNING YOUR TRIP **Getting there** Naples Airport is the nearest to the coast. **Getting around** A rental car is the best way to explore the Amalfi Coast. **Weather** Days are sunny and warm with some showers. Temperatures dip at night. **Average temperature** 61°F / 16°C.

BOSTON

North America US
BOSTON

WHY GO *With the start of the baseball season, the Boston Marathon, and basketball and ice hockey games in full swing, this is the month to join the crowds of adoring sports fanatics in Massachusetts' enigmatic capital.*

Historic and homey, Boston is a city of quiet charm and tradition, but the revolutionary citadel positively pulses in April, as fans descend on Bean Town for a month of all-American sports. From early April, crowds fill the iconic Fenway Park stadium to support the beloved Red Sox, the metallic smack of baseball bats against balls punctuating the cheers of the devoted crowds. Basketball buffs, meanwhile, watch the Boston Celtics dribble their way around the impressive TD Garden, a space shared with the Boston Bruins ice hockey team. Even those who don't enjoy competitive sports will find it hard to resist the inspiring sight of 30,000

dedicated runners pounding the city streets for the Boston Marathon on the third Monday of the month.

Sports aside, Boston's pretty neighborhoods cry out to be explored. The town houses and cobbled streets of Beacon Hill, topped with gaslit Louisburg Square, are the perfectly preserved Boston of the 1840s. Sculls and sailboats glide by on the Charles River, joggers and skaters puff past on the Esplanade, and students make the place a lively city of eternal youth, filled with cafés, quirky bookshops, and fashion boutiques. A visit to the city wouldn't be complete without frequenting the city's pubs, including Cheers on Beacon Hill, which inspired the TV

series of the same name. After a few nights enjoying traditional hospitality, you'll relish the fresh sea breezes afforded by some New England island-hopping.

When Else to Go
September Food festivals and fall colors galore. **December** Quieter, chillier, and festive.

PLANNING YOUR TRIP **Getting there** Logan International Aiport is 3 miles (5 km) from the city center. **Getting around** Boston is compact and walkable, but you can also use the MBTA subway. **Weather** Warm and pleasant. **Average temperature** 63°F / 17°C.

Clockwise from top
Attractive town houses
and trees lining Mount
Vernon Street, Beacon Hill;
sun rising over Fenway Park;
Hanley Ramirez batting for
the Boston Red Sox

// MAY

Boats moored on the
ethereal Lake Windermere
in England's Lake District

The sun setting over a hillside peppered with bluebells in Rannerdale, the Lake District

LAKE DISTRICT

Europe England
LAKE DISTRICT

WHY GO *May brings longer, milder days and an abundance of wildlife to the Lake District. Get your hiking boots on and follow bluebell trails, amble through fields of frolicking lambs, and climb the region's famous fells.*

Spring is in full bloom in the Lake District, a region famous for its wild, natural beauty. The landscape was immortalized in the works of William Wordsworth and Beatrix Potter, and today draws walkers looking to climb the likes of Scafell Pike, the highest summit in England at 3,210 ft (978 m).

For a trail less traveled, consider the 4-mile (6-km) stretch from Rannerdale to Buttermere, which is doable in just three hours. Following a series of paths, you'll catch sight of the region's native Herdwick sheep and smatterings of bluebells in the fields at this time of year. Rannerdale Knotts stands at 1,165 ft (355 m), making for a relatively easy ascent. As you wind your way through the lowland valleys, craggy fells rise above you, splashed with burnt orange, emerald green,

and earthy brown hues. The path is a little steep toward the top of Rannerdale Knotts, so pause on a boulder and listen to the streams trickling down the hillsides and the distant trills of bleating lambs. Continue on to the peak, where you'll be well rewarded with beautiful views out over the North Western Fells.

You've earned a hearty meal after all that hiking. Follow the path back down to the village of Buttermere and tuck into lunch at one of the historic pubs. By the end of the route, you'll have experienced spring in all its glory.

When Else to Go

July–August Summer welcomes agricultural shows and beer festivals.
November Join the locals in towns and villages for Bonfire Night.

PLANNING YOUR TRIP **Getting there** The Lake District is in the northeastern county of Cumbria. There are regular trains from London Euston to Oxenholme, and from here you can catch a train on to larger towns. **Getting around** A car is strongly advised. Walking and cycling are great ways to explore. **Weather** Days are generally dry, though layers are recommended because it can be brisk. **Average temperature** 54°F / 12°C.

BEST PLACES TO RECHARGE

The English countryside springs to life in May. After a day spent embracing the great outdoors, indulge in some well-earned rest and relaxation.

Ambleside Wind down in style in Zeffrelli's, a Mediterranean-inspired restaurant and jazz bar that even has its own independent theater—opt for the meal-and-movie combo and sink into those plush red seats.

Coniston Away from Coniston's Yewdale Fells is Yew Tree Farm, a quaint B&B where Beatrix Potter resided during the 1930s. Soak up the ambience in the outdoor hot tub.

Windermere Go glamping in Windermere's stunning Low Wray. At this National Trust-owned campsite, you can rest in a fully furnished safari tent or curl up in a luxury treetop pod.

Cartmel For a spot of afternoon tea, head to Cartmel's award-winning Hazelmere Café. There's a strong focus on using local produce, from Cumberland sausages to Morecambe Bay shrimps.

Grasmere Sample world-famous Grasmere gingerbread *(below)* at the 1854-established Grasmere Gingerbread Shop, before visiting William Wordsworth's grave.

PRAGUE

Europe *Czech Republic*
PRAGUE

WHY GO *By day, enjoy the city sights; by night, the Prague Spring concerts. This really is the best time to visit.*

Mozart once said, "My orchestra is in Prague," and during the city's legendary Spring music festival, it appears that every great orchestra in the world has joined it. Since 1946, the festival has hosted only the world's very best performance artists, symphony orchestras, and chamber music ensembles, all performing in Prague's first-rate venues.

The finest of them is the Obecní Dům (Municipal House), completed in 1911: a concert hall, ballroom, café, and restaurant with such a whimsical and exuberant design that the 15th-century Powder Gate next to it appears almost offended at the flamboyant upstart. In the Smetana Hall, at the building's core, the ornate decoration leaves the concertgoer breathless and doubtful that any performer could live up to such surroundings. Time and again, however, conductors and soloists find themselves inspired to outdo the setting. This mix produces arguably the greatest series of annual concerts in Europe.

When Else to Go
December Wrap up warm and get festive at Prague's wonderful Christmas markets.

PLANNING YOUR TRIP **Getting there** Václav Havel Airport is 6 miles (10 km) from the center. **Getting around** Prague's compact center is walkable, but there is a reliable bus and tram network. **Weather** Usually sunny with minimal rainfall. **Average temperature** 64°F / 18°C.

South America Bolivia
LA PAZ

LA PAZ

WHY GO *May is an ideal time to visit La Paz and its surrounding area since the weather is pleasant and mild.*

Thanks to the altitude and spectacular setting of Bolivia's de facto capital city, those arriving by air will enjoy a breathtaking introduction to La Paz. The international airport sits on the lung-stifling 13,125 ft (4,000 m) high Altiplano, the windswept plain that dominates southwestern Bolivia.

While the altitude, elevation, and crowds make La Paz physically challenging to explore on foot, there's no better way to immerse yourself in the sights, sounds, and smells of this distinctly Andean metropolis. More than half of the city's population is of Aymara or Quechua heritage, and *cholas*—indigenous women wearing long braids and clad in bowler hats and multilayered dresses—crowd the bustling footpaths, street corners, and local markets, selling everything from *empanadas* to local medicine. *"Comprame"* (buy from me), they call out to shoppers threading through the maze of vendors, hoping to engage them in a session of spirited haggling.

Accompanied by the incessant din of horn-blaring traffic, this scene is the essence of the La Paz experience—but respite isn't far. There are plenty of quiet coffee shops and diverse museums, and the city's spectacular hinterlands offer even greater scope for relaxation.

When Else to Go
June Celebrate Aymara New Year on the winter solstice.

PLANNING YOUR TRIP **Getting there** La Paz is served by El Alto International Airport. **Getting around** Travel by inexpensive taxi, *trufi* (collective taxis), *colectivos* (collective minibuses), and *micros* (buses). **Weather** Dry, mild days and cool evenings. **Average temperature** 60°F / 18°C.

Two women, dressed in traditional clothing, outside a market in La Paz

ZAMBIA

VICTORIA
FALLS

ZIMBABWE

Africa Zambia and Zimbabwe
VICTORIA FALLS

WHY GO *Victoria Falls is a year-round destination, but May is the perfect month to come. The summer rains are over, but the falls are at full flow, with rainbows common.*

Undoubtedly one of the world's great natural wonders, there's nothing to prepare visitors for the majesty of Victoria Falls, or Mosi-oa-Tunya ("the smoke that thunders"). At their widest, the falls measure more than 5,578 ft (1,700 m) and at their highest 355 ft (108 m)—the largest in the world, almost twice as wide and deep as North America's Niagara.

Victoria Falls, named by David Livingstone after the Queen of the United Kingdom, straddles an international border and demonstrates two distinct personalities. In Zimbabwe, the falls remain at a distance, viewed across the gorge from a lush rain forest park created by the perpetually thick mist that's pumped out by the falling water. A more intimate relationship with the falls is available on the Zambian side. Here, visitors can saunter right up to the lip where the Zambezi plunges over the edge or negotiate a series of mist-soaked trails and catwalks.

This contrasting nature is also evident in the two border towns. Although Zimbabwe's reputation has suffered, Victoria Falls town thrives regardless of the country's economic and political troubles. Saturated with hotels, guesthouses, steak joints, casinos, and tour agencies, it is fueled by tourism. Zambia, meanwhile, is enjoying the fruits of its political reforms and is fast developing a tourist scene of its own—with less of the commercialism evident across the border.

Whichever side you choose, once you've seen the falls, there's still plenty to do. Get soaked on a raft trip through the gorges or a micro-light flight through the mist; enjoy a cruise on the hippo- and croc-infested river. Photograph elephants, antelope, and lions on a safari; try rock climbing; or just relax with a cold Zambezi Lager and toast the good fortune that brought you to Africa.

When Else to Go
September Come when the waters are lower to swim in the ultimate infinity pool, the Devil's Pool, with views over the waterfall's edge.

PLANNING YOUR TRIP **Getting there** Fly into Victoria Falls or Harry Mwanga Nkumbula International airports. **Getting around** Taxis from either side of the falls will get you to the respective border posts; the no-man's land between the two posts requires a walk or change of taxi. **Weather** Warm and sunny. **Average temperature** 82°F / 28°C.

"Undoubtedly one of the world's great natural wonders, there's nothing to prepare visitors for the majesty of Victoria Falls."

Mist rising from the simply awesome Victoria Falls, or Mosi-oa-Tunya, in Southern Africa

BALI

Right The lush rice terraces of Tegallalang, in central Bali, viewed from the air

Below A bowl of healthy fruit for breakfast; meditating by a swimming pool at sunset

Asia Indonesia
BALI

WHY GO *May brings clear skies and welcome respite from the tropical storms of Bali's rainy season. Visit in May, too, to avoid the summer crowds.*

The island of Bali, nestled within the Indonesian Archipelago, is one of the world's most relaxing vacation destinations. Exotic and diverse, the island is picturesque to the point of resembling a painted backdrop—volcanoes climb into clouds and terraced rice fields cascade down to the ocean. Bali blends its beautiful nature with a mind-bogglingly impressive concentration of spas. These spas— timeless havens of serenity—are dedicated not only to pampering the body but also to restoring inner equilibrium and are therefore a magnet for those in search of something that will ease fatigue, stimulate the senses, and awaken the spirit. Here, you can practice yoga, soothe tired muscles with a traditional Boreh treatment, or simply unplug from it all and relax in near paradise.

When Else to Go
June–July Time your visit with the much-celebrated Bali Arts Festival to see dance shows, concerts, art exhibitions, and more.

PLANNING YOUR TRIP **Getting there** Bali is served by Ngurah Rai International Airport (Denpasar). **Getting around** Use air-conditioned taxis or hire a vehicle with a driver, or rent your own car or motorcycle. **Weather** May comes early in Bali's dry season. Expect sunshine, though the mountainous regions can be cooler. **Average temperature** 86°F / 30°C.

FIRTH OF CLYDE

Left A picture-postcard cottage in Glencoe, west Scotland

Below Getting up close to a Highland cow; an actor dressed as Robert Burns standing outside the cottage where the poet was born

Europe Scotland
WEST COAST

WHY GO *Festival season hits west Scotland, with the biggest celebrations taking place during Burns An' A' That!*

The sun sinks slowly to the horizon, a golden red orb lighting liquid gold ripples across the darkening Firth of Clyde. As it disappears behind the islands and the glow fades, the night sky is suddenly alive with a brilliance of color. People crowd onto Ayr's Low Green while others line the promenade along the beach, enjoying the fireworks and the music that is the finale of the Burns An' A' That! festival, a celebration of the life and works of Scotland's most famous poet, Robert Burns, as well as a showcase for contemporary Scottish culture. For ten days, the country has been awash with readings, tastings, concerts, walks, and storytelling. If Burns were alive today, there is no doubt he would be with the musicians in the pubs, swapping stories and joining the crowds for the fireworks.

Once the celebrations are over, make your way up the west coast. Wind your way past tiny picturesque fishing villages and spectacular dramatic glens, savoring undisturbed views that might inspire you to write some poetry of your own.

When Else to Go
September–October The departure of the summer crowds and the changing colors of the landscape herald a new season.

PLANNING YOUR TRIP **Getting there** Ayr is 37 miles (60 km) southwest of Glasgow, accessible via Glasgow International Airport. **Getting around** The practical way to tour the west is by car. **Weather** Wet and mild with sunny days. **Average temperature** 57°F / 14°C.

COLORADO
PLATEAU

North America US
COLORADO PLATEAU

WHY GO *The Colorado Plateau is pleasantly warm in late May, perfect for hiking and long drives. The parks are at their greenest and the summer crowds are yet to arrive.*

Quite simply, the Colorado Plateau is home to some of the most jaw-dropping examples of landscapes to be found anywhere in the world. Dreamlike spires of rock and delicate wind-carved arches stand in silence above stunning desert tableaux, while ancient rivers run through mile-deep canyons whose towering red-rock walls hold a record of the past 50 million years or so. Some landscapes, such as the buttes and mesas of Monument Valley, have appeared in countless films, making them instantly recognizable. Others, like Zion's river-carved canyon, are startlingly new and fresh. Even the Grand Canyon offers refreshing vistas when viewed from the North Rim. More than 1,000 ft (305 m) higher than the more famous and desertlike South Rim, the North Rim is blanketed in cool green forest, and from the canyon edge, the Colorado River appears as an almost-hidden glimmer thousands of feet below.

The region's spectacular wilderness is inevitably perfect for exploring on foot. Discover hidden desert sanctuaries, where translucent green pools are fed by misty waterfalls, and weirdly wonderful landscapes of red stone towers, sculpted by the wind. On the Rim Trail, wander for mile upon mile along the edge of the truly epic Grand Canyon.

One of the very best ways to travel around the region is in an RV, which offers unparalleled freedom to explore at your own pace. There is nothing like enjoying a coffee in the early morning crispness of the desert air and anticipating the day's adventure ahead.

When Else to Go
September–October Temperatures drop after the heat of summer.

PLANNING YOUR TRIP **Getting there** Fly into Las Vegas airport, well served by international and domestic airlines, then drive. **Getting around** Travel by RV or car. **Weather** Sunny, warm days and cool evenings. **Average temperature** 72°F / 22°C.

HIKES AROUND THE PLATEAU

1 **Bighorn Canyon**, found in the Grand Staircase-Escalante National Monument, is one of the easier hikes, at 7.8 miles (12.5 km).

2 **Phipps Wash** is a lovely 8.6-mile (13.8-km) hike in the Grand Staircase-Escalante National Monument. There is a small amount of scrabbling, but it's worth it for the great views atop Maverick Bridge.

3 **Salt Creek**, in the Needles District of Canyonlands National Park, has cliff dwellings and petroglyphs—reminders of the region's Ancestral Puebloan culture. At 24 miles (39 km), it's a longer hike, and you'll need to look into backcountry camping.

4 **Professor Creek**, a short distance from Moab, is a really refreshing hike, as it involves paddling in shallow streams and concludes at a double-tongued waterfall. It lasts for 8 miles (13 km).

5 **The Rim Trail**, which stretches for some 13 miles (21 km) around Grand Canyon National Park, is straight-forward with fabulous vistas (*below*).

Gazing at the
awe-inspiring
geology of Antelope
Canyon, a slot
canyon found in
northern Arizona

CRETE

Europe Greece
CRETE

WHY GO *Crete's summer begins with warm May days when the lowlands are draped with colorful wildflowers.*

Crucible of ancient civilizations, Crete is packed with archaeological treasures, yet it is the natural landscape that shines at this time of year. The island is wonderfully alive, with dark green olive trees, fragrant orange groves, and pink oleander growing wild.

There's good walking here, most famously the Samaria Gorge, a demanding hike to the south coast and one of the most striking areas of natural beauty in Greece. Easier is the Therisso Gorge, threaded by a tiny road and edged by wildflowers. From high on the hills you are almost transported to the distant past.

When Else to Go
March Experience the exuberant carnival celebrations in Rethymno and Irakleio.

PLANNING YOUR TRIP Getting there Crete is an island south of Athens, with three airports: Irakleio, Chania, and Sita. **Getting around** Travel by bus, taxi, or rental car. **Weather** Warm and sunny. **Average temperature** 77°F / 25°C.

The small village of Sfakia, fringed by hills, on the island's south coast

Asia China
SILK ROAD

WHY GO *A journey along the Silk Road continues to capture the imagination of travelers. Take your trip in May to avoid the extreme heat of summer.*

Few routes compare to the epic Silk Road. Traversing some 4,300 miles (7,000 km), this ancient trading route was not a single highway but a network of routes converging and diverging across Asia. Xi'an was the beginning of the north route, and it still makes a good starting point for a memorable trip of your own. Each leg of the route is a matter of minutes by plane, but taking the train is recommended if you have the time—the sense of journey is much better captured watching the changing landscape and architecture through a train car window.

The Silk Road has countless highlights. In Xi'an, see the majestic Big Wild Goose Pagoda and visit the extraordinary site of the Terracotta Army; witness Jiayuguan's imposing fort, a magnificent piece of architectural drama; and stop in Dunhuang to explore the Mogao Caves, the richest collection of Buddhist art in China. Out of your train window, gaze at decorative mosques, dusty desert, and mountain scenery. This trip is raucous, dusty, hot, unmissable—but what more could you want?

When Else to Go
September–October After the heat of summer, the temperature drops and fall colors come into play. Avoid the blazing hot summers and bitterly cold winters.

PLANNING YOUR TRIP Getting there Xi'an is served by an international airport, though many visitors arrive via Beijing. **Getting around** The most rewarding way to see the region is by train. **Weather** Mild and springlike. **Average temperature** 74°F / 23°C.

Clockwise from top left A mural in the Mogao Caves; the mountainous landscape of Xinjiang; Jiayuguan's elaborate fort; the terra-cotta warriors in Xi'an; Crescent Lake, an oasis near Dunhuang; a man selling rugs at a local bazaar

A city of contrasts: the streets of New York's Lower Manhattan and the sleek skyscrapers towering beyond

NEW YORK CITY

North America US
NEW YORK CITY

WHY GO *One of the world's most exciting cities, New York is full of cultural riches—art, theater, museums—alongside world-class food and shopping. Late spring is a great time to visit, with mild days and a few festivals, including the Tribeca Film Festival.*

The pulse and the pace are daunting at first, but the relentlessly fast rhythm of city life can't be ignored. Before you know it, you're dashing around like a local, eating on the run and sharing in the excitement. New York can be anything you want it to be: stylishly chic or cutting-edge trendy; a high temple of culture or a hive of commercialism.

Exploring is an unending pleasure because every neighborhood offers a different mood and architecture, from the dazzle of Broadway neon and the cast-iron landmarks of SoHo to the glittering skyscrapers of the Financial District. The best way to see it all is on foot. Stroll the Upper East Side for Beaux-Arts mansions and dozens of museums, including the Frick Collection, Frank Lloyd Wright's landmark Guggenheim, and the Jewish Museum. Head to the Upper West Side for classic Art Deco apartments and even more museums.

To really feel the flavor of the city, share some other favorite pleasures with New Yorkers. Watch street performers and the passing parade of city folk from the steps of the Metropolitan Museum of Art on weekend afternoons. Browse the stalls of the farmers' Greenmarket in Union Square. Walk the East River Promenade from Brookfield Place through Battery Park, with the Statue of Liberty in view all the way. Take in a show or check out Sunday's GreenFlea market at Columbus Avenue and 77th Street. You'll quickly understand why so many love calling the Big Apple home.

When Else to Go
June Join the party during Pride and at the Puerto Rican Day Parade.
December Christmas celebrations kick off with lights and decorations aplenty.

PLANNING YOUR TRIP **Getting there** New York is served by three airports: LaGuardia (domestic), JFK, and Newark. **Getting around** New York is a great city to tour on foot. The subway system is comprehensive. **Weather** May is usually sunny, though there can be cold spells, so pack plenty of layers. **Average temperature** 72°F / 20°C.

// JUNE

The dramatic volcanic
landscape near Askja
caldera, Iceland

Above Gridded streets surrounding the unfinished Sagrada Família, designed by Antoni Gaudí

Right A firestarter performing for the Night of Fire; partygoers enjoying a performance at Sónar music festival

BARCELONA

Europe Spain
BARCELONA

WHY GO *As well as offering Barcelona's best weather, June has a cultural calendar chock-full of festivals and events. The highlight is the huge all-night celebration Sant Joan, when partygoers flock to the beach in droves.*

Nestled between the Mediterranean and the two mountains of Montjuïc and Tibidabo, Barcelona is a naturally theatrical city. Along La Rambla—a spectacular mile-long promenade that connects the city to the sea—everyone is part of the performance, and tourists join the human statues, dancers, and other entertainers who form the resident cast. Winding streets lead off into the Barri Gòtic, the city's medieval core, with its columned churches, shaded doorways, elaborate gargoyles, and tiny alleys that suddenly open up onto romantic squares and sunstruck courtyards. In the Born district, medieval palaces now house art museums and lively tapas and cava bars, while cutting-edge design shops

and chic modern restaurants stand alongside the city's coolest clubs.

Mid-June sees the Sónar music festival, a three-day celebration of electronic sound and digital art and innovation. However, the real highlight of the month is Sant Joan, the "Night of Fire," on June 23, when Barcelona is framed by giant fireworks displays on the surrounding hillsides. Revelers gather on the beach to dance the night away around huge bonfires, before greeting the new dawn with a bracing swim.

When Else to Go
September As the summer draws to a close, enjoy parades and parties at the Fiesta de la Mercè.

PLANNING YOUR TRIP **Getting there** The international airport, El Prat, is connected to the city center by bus, train, and taxi. **Getting around** The city is easily explored on foot, and there are excellent bus and metro connections. **Weather** Reliably sunny; rain is unusual. **Average temperature** 77°F / 25°C.

Avant-garde and achingly cool, Barcelona has something for every hour of the day.

1 **Gaudí architecture** is wonderfully whimsical. Pay homage to the genius at Casa Batllo, Park Güell, and—of course—the Sagrada Família.

2 **La Rambla** is the beating heart of the city, a thrumming thoroughfare where locals come to eat, drink, and catch up with friends.

3 **Barcelona's nightlife** is second to none. Neighborhoods like El Raval, El Born, and Eixample are chock-full of bars and clubs.

4 **Museums** cover everything from modern art and design to the history of the city. Culture vultures won't know where to begin.

5 **Montjuïc** rises over the city with its fortress, gardens, and Olympic Park. Buy a bottle of cava, catch the cable car to the top, and enjoy the view.

TOP TIP

You'll find the perfect photo spot at Carrer de l'Allada-Vermell 12, in El Born. Potted plants and leafy shrubs line this gorgeously weathered apartment.

YUNNAN

Asia China
YUNNAN

WHY GO *In June, Yunnan's Tiger Leaping Gorge is swollen with rainfall, making it the perfect time to embark on a dramatic gorge walk.*

Tiger Leaping Gorge is one of China's great natural wonders. Here, the Jinsha-Jiang, the River of Golden Sand, slices its way through two 16,400 ft (5,000 m) high peaks, Jade Dragon Snow Mountain and Haba Snow Mountain. As you hike along the narrow ridge that traces the mountainside, far below the river rages, while high above, the cloud-draped mountain soars. Each turn reveals another sublime view—it's no wonder that those completing this 20-mile (32 km) gorge trek complain of tired necks as well as knees.

When Else to Go
April Spring sees the Water Splashing Festival, which celebrates the new year in Xishuangbana.

PLANNING YOUR TRIP Getting there The Yunnan region is served by Kunming Changshui International Airport and intercity buses. **Getting around** Taxis are plentiful and cheap. **Weather** Mild and clear. **Average temperature** 66°F / 19°C.

The flooded Jinsha River carving its way through Tiger Leaping Gorge in a huge torrent of water

North America Canada
MONTREAL

WHY GO *Montreal is a hotbed of fun in summer, and the International Jazz Festival is its shining star.*

MONTREAL

The Canadian summer is sweet and desperately short, but Montrealers are experts at making the most of it. When the snow melts, the city erupts into a seamless riot of festivals, street parties, and celebrations. Any excuse will suffice: hand in a request, cordon off a sleepy *rue,* and the jubilation begins. The best is the *Festival International de Jazz,* held from late June to early July. Conceived as a festival for the *peuple,* it's a 10-day extravaganza of 500 concerts held at open-air venues (free), music halls, and jazz clubs. Just about everyone comes, with crowds of around two million people gathering together to enjoy the music. Legendary jazz players from all over the world line up to join in and share a stage with the local talent, making the festival one of the best parties on the planet.

Montreal is like a jazz piece itself—it will surprise you at every turn. This dynamic city tries to be most things to most people—with culture, nightlife, and shopping galore—and, with Gallic flair, it always succeeds.

When Else to Go
February Check out La Poutine Week, an extravaganza of chips, cheese curds, and gravy.

PLANNING YOUR TRIP **Getting there** Trudeau International Airport is a half-hour taxi ride from the city center. **Getting around** The metro and bus network are the most efficient ways to get around. **Weather** Showers are frequent but pass quickly. **Average temperature** 68°F / 20°C.

A jazz band performing on the main stage during the *Festival International de Jazz*

Numerous kitsch signs for honky-tonk bars along Broadway's bustling sidewalk in down-town Nashville

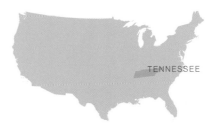

North America US
TENNESSEE

WHY GO *For four magical days in June, hundreds of the best country music stars descend on Nashville, while Memphis rocks to the beat.*

Music, music, and more music! Where else in the world can you find two cities renowned for their musical styles just a half day's drive from each other? Nashville is the home of country, and every June the city hosts the star-studded Country Music Association (CMA) Festival. For four days, the city is one big party, so jump into the concert crowds, throw your hands up high, dance to the music, and lip-sync the words to your favorite songs.

If Nashville is the polished center of country, Memphis is the down-home town that cooked up rhythm-and-blues and rock and roll. Sun Records—where Johnny Cash and a kid named Elvis got their start—is R&B's fountainhead, but Graceland is its heart. Spend a night hitting the bars of Beale Street where you'll dig into steaming plates of gumbo, drink ice-cold beer, and dance to some of the best blues in America.

When Else to Go
May The Beale Street Music Festival and the Blues Music Awards get Memphis pumping.

PLANNING YOUR TRIP Getting there Nashville and Memphis both have international airports, but Memphis offers more flights. **Getting around** Rent a car at either airport. The drive between the two cities takes four hours. **Weather** Warm and humid. **Average temperature** 90°F / 32°C.

ULURU

Oceania Australia
ULURU

WHY GO *This mystical red rock speaks to the soul. Visit in June, when the temperature is at its most forgiving, and try to catch the full moon rising up from behind Uluru at sunset.*

Approaching the enormous monolith of Uluru, you cannot help but be awestruck by the spectacle of this terra-cotta giant—the oldest temple in the world—looming over the endless desert landscape. Don't let the word "desert" fool you; the Uluru-Kata Tjuta National Park teems with wildlife and flora. Desert she-oak trees dot the landscape and birds of crimson and gold dance beneath them, feasting on flowering plants. At night, the howl of a dingo echoes eerily across the red sand.

As you tackle the four-hour trail around Uluru's circumference, you'll be constantly surprised by water holes and ancient rock art. Time your walk to end just before sunset, then settle at one of the viewing spots to see the incredible colors that peel away from the rock as the sun drops behind it.

With a 4WD vehicle, the horizon of this vast wilderness is limitless.

Marvel at the high walls of Ormiston Gorge as you walk along the riverbed. Float on your back in the Ellery Creek water hole, gazing at the ochre cliffs above. Camp among ghost gums by the Finke River, towered over by the elegant palms of Palm Valley. And don't miss Kata Tjuta—an otherworldly group of 36 domes, with gorges and valleys so hauntingly quiet that they evoke the huge spiritual significance of this strange landscape.

A few days in the red center will change your concept of time forever. Forget your watch, for it's impossible to measure the eons of creation evident in this ancient land.

When Else to Go
September–October Spring is a great time to visit Uluru, with comfortable temperatures and (relatively) little rain making for perfect walking and cycling conditions.

Above Uluru, set against a pink-hued sky, at dawn

Right Colorful designs on didgeridoos; pink mulla mulla flowering in the desert; ancient Aboriginal rock painting showing a hunter and a kangaroo

PLANNING YOUR TRIP Getting there There are daily domestic flights to Alice Springs and Ayers Rock Airport, and from nearby Yulara you can take the shuttle to Uluru. **Getting around** Rent a car in Alice Springs to explore the area. **Weather** Pleasant during the day, but temperatures at night can drop to 42°F / 5°C. **Average temperature** 66°F / 19°C.

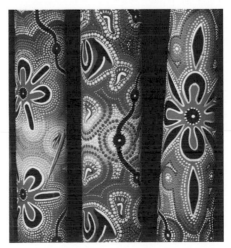

ICELAND

Europe
ICELAND

WHY GO *With around-the-clock daylight, there's plenty of opportunity to experience all that this country has to offer, from its eponymous ice to its natural heat.*

Nearly everything ever written about Iceland refers to it as "the land of fire and ice," and for good reason—although it is a rather tired old moniker, these natural forces represent some of the island's greatest assets. Iceland literally lives and breathes geology, from sheep pastures nurtured by the rich, volcanic soil and sparkling glacial runoff to the distinctly aromatic geothermal heat and energy that powers the country. Its expansive glaciers, active volcanoes, hot springs, geysers, lonely mountains, wild rivers, and innumerable waterfalls will awe every traveler.

From May to July, the island is bathed in around-the-clock sub-Arctic daylight (notwithstanding a good measure of North Atlantic rain). You may find Iceland's prices rather high, but you can take solace in the fact that for the money, you'll be getting two days in one. As the children of the Vikings discovered long ago, that's twice the time to indulge in Iceland's decadent offerings. Trot across the moors on a horse, walk on a lonely white icefield, soothe your skin in the mineral-rich waters of the Blue Lagoon, or defeat the cold, drenching rain with an open-air soak in a hot tub. And by the time you've headed back into Reykjavík, it'll still be light enough for plenty of eating, drinking, and merriment. Or if you're tough enough, the Reykjavík *rúntur*—an all-night pub crawl under the midnight sun.

When Else to Go
September–October Before the brutal cold of midwinter arrives (though it'll still be very chilly), this is the peak time for spotting the dazzling Northern Lights.

Striking Mount Kirkjufell, and the Kirkjufellsfoss waterfalls, near the town of Grundarfjörður

PLANNING YOUR TRIP Getting there Flights arrive into Keflavík International Airport, 30 miles (50 km) west of Reykjavík. **Getting around** Rent a car or use the public bus system. For sights farther afield, use bus tours. **Weather** Predominantly wet, with some rain-free days. **Average temperature** 48°F / 9°C.

VANCOUVER

HALIFAX

North America Canada
COAST TO COAST

WHY GO *Summer arrives in June, bringing with it longer days, warmer temperatures, and a greater chance of glimpsing Canada's famous wildlife—perfect for this spectacular journey.*

The twin ribbons of steel that stretch for thousands of miles across Canada have tales to tell of the travelers who have made history on this journey—mounties and military men, pioneers and poets. Built in the 1880s, these rails united a nation, weaving together the threads of a landscape as varied as the people. It's still an epic route today, following the mighty St. Lawrence River to the granite outcroppings of the Canadian Shield, across the great prairie plains and through pine and spruce trees in the Rockies, and emerging from rain forests to greet the Pacific Ocean.

Ride the rails from sea to sea and you'll glimpse the old stories, set against the rhythmic sway of the train.

In the Rockies, among the sawtoothed peaks and dramatic mountains, tales tell of the explorers who found the first routes through treacherous mountain passes and the thousands of workers who built high, heart-in-mouth bridges and long tunnels into unforgiving rock.

Many travelers choose a small portion of the cross-Canada route, but the intrepid can cross the entire nation by rail between Halifax and Vancouver. So settle back in your seat, relax, and let the scenes unfold outside your window. This trip is all about the journey.

When Else to Go
October As fall arrives, forests are awash with fiery reds and oranges.

PLANNING YOUR TRIP **Getting there** Flights arrive into all major cities, including Halifax (at Stanfield International Airport). **Getting around** You can travel either east- or westbound by train, starting in Halifax or Vancouver. **Weather** Mild and humid, with cool evenings. **Average temperature** 68°F / 20°C.

WILDLIFE ENCOUNTERS

Few things can match the excitement of seeing Canada's awesome animals in the wild. Here are a few highlights.

1 **Bears** Grizzly, black, and brown bears are found in the Rockies' national parks and remote areas, although sightings are rare.

2 **Bald eagles** From the train window, keep an eye out for the distinctive white head and white tail of a bald eagle, Canada's largest bird of prey.

3 **Moose** Canada has about one million of these solitary creatures, with their massive muzzles and broad antlers, so you're likely to see at least one.

4 **Osprey** This huge bird of prey lives all over Canada. Their massive nests can be seen perched on top of dead trees or hydro poles.

5 **Whales** Canada's coastal waters are home to various species of whales. These gentle giants are often close enough to shore to be seen from land.

TOP TIP

Vancouver Island offers some of the best opportunities to see whales. From March to August, daily whale-watching trips depart from Tofino, Ucluelet, and Bamfield. The huge humpback whale is the easiest to spot.

"Settle back in your seat, relax, and let the scenes unfold outside your window. This trip is all about the journey."

Clockwise from top Passing through Banff National Park in the Rockies; admiring the incredible scenery through a train carriage window; the sun setting over Peggy's Cove lighthouse in Nova Scotia, near Halifax

MACHU PICCHU

South America Peru
MACHU PICCHU

WHY GO *With clear skies and fine weather for hiking, June is when the true magic of the Salkantay trek unfolds. This route is also a great alternative to the oversubscribed Inca Trail.*

As you tread the stony trail, the glacier-saddled peak of Nevado Salkantay rears into the cobalt-blue sky. One of the most venerated by the Inca Empire, it now forms the backdrop for the region's most compelling trek, the eponymous Salkantay. Although reaching Machu Picchu is the route's main aim, the 45-mile (72-km) trail is as much about the journey as reaching the final destination.

Trekking through snow-dusted Andean landscapes, you traverse 15 different ecosystems. Purple lupins line the path, while cyan lakes are encircled by glaciated peaks. At the trek's highest point, the Salkantay Pass, you'll see the *apachetas*, small piles of stone made as offerings to the mountain spirits. At lower altitudes, the humid cloud forest guards vivid orchids and flitting hummingbirds. Keep your eyes peeled for the playful cock-of-the-rock, with its vibrant orange plumage.

Dawn on the final day breaks with the mist rolling off the mountains to reveal a stone city of exquisite agricultural terraces and ceremonial temples—welcome to Machu Picchu. Saddled between two mountain peaks in the subtropical Andean foothills, this fortress was intended to be appreciated as just one part of its spectacular natural setting. Take the perilous ascent up Huayna Picchu, the peak directly behind the city, where dizzying views of the entire complex and the serrated mountains beyond are an apt conclusion to your adventure.

When Else to Go
April and September The shoulder months promise fewer tourists and lusher scenery, with occasional rain showers triggering a bloom of vibrant wildflowers.

PLANNING YOUR TRIP **Getting there** Fly from Lima International Airport to Cusco. The Salkantay trek begins from Sallapata, 62 miles (100 km) and a three-hour drive from Cusco; transportation to this point is through an organized tour or public transportation. **Getting around** A five-day organized tour is the easiest way to experience the trek. **Weather** Dry and sunny, with cold nights. **Average temperature** 68°F / 20°C.

EXPERIENCE INCA PERU

The Inca Empire left behind a trail of magnificent ancient treasures throughout the Andes. Machu Picchu might be the jewel in the region's crown, but a host of lesser-known remains and experiences beckon, allowing you to follow in the footsteps of the Incas.

1 Bustling **Andean markets** sell much the same vegetables as they did in Inca times.

2 Held in honor of the Sun God, **Inti Raymi** is a lively Inca festival celebrated on the winter solstice.

3 In June, a festival is held to repair the amazing **Q'eswachaka**, a rope bridge across the Río Apurimac.

4 The **Inca Jungle Trek** is a blend of thrilling activities and hiking—perfect for adventure lovers.

5 Embark on the challenging two-day hike to **Choquequirao**, a lesser-known Inca fortress.

Mist rising off the ruins of Machu Picchu, one of South America's most evocative and breathtaking sights

Europe Italy
ROME

WHY GO *June is the start of the revered* Estate Romana. *During this summer festival, eclectic events are held at outdoor venues across the city, from the Imperial Forum and Villa Borghese to dozens of parks and piazzas.*

The eternal city has been attracting visitors for centuries. Some come to witness the glories of ancient Rome—the magnificent Forum, the Colosseum, and the Palatine Hill. Others come to gaze up at the beautiful ceiling of the Vatican's Sistine Chapel, to browse covetously in the designer shops on the Via dei Condotti, or simply to feast on the local cuisine—thin and crispy wood-fired pizzas, any of a hundred delicious pasta dishes, or lightly fried zucchini flowers—the ultimate taste of summer. And to finish, some homemade *gelato*.

Whatever the reason for your visit, you can't walk far without stumbling upon something extraordinary, whether it's the *Area Sacra*, where the remains of ancient temples and the rumored site of Caesar's assassination sit in the middle of a noisy square, or Bernini's flamboyant sculptures cavorting in the fountains of the Piazza Navona. Rome has been called a living museum, but it is also very much a living city. Strolling through the old Jewish quarter or around the Campo de' Fiori, peeking into the artisans' workshops that line neighborhood streets, or exploring the alleys of the bohemian Trastevere district gives a delightful insight into Roman life.

When Else to Go
April Spring in the Italian capital sees mild temperatures, fewer visitors than in the summer, and all manner of Easter festivities.

PLANNING YOUR TRIP Getting there Rome has two airports: Leonardo da Vinci (Fiumicino) is connected to the city by train, Ciampino by bus. **Getting around** Rome is easily navigable on foot or by metro, bus, and tram. **Weather** Little chance of rain. **Average temperature** 82°F / 28°C.

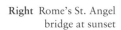

Right Rome's St. Angel bridge at sunset

Below The Roman Colosseum, the largest amphitheater ever built

"Some come to witness the glories of ancient Rome—the magnificent Forum, the Colosseum, and the Palatine Hill."

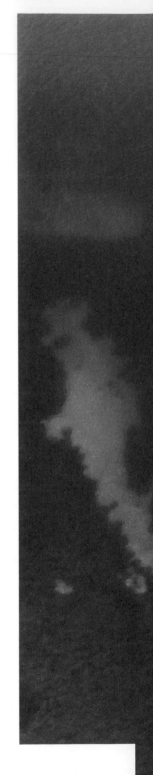

DALMATIAN COAST

Europe Croatia
DALMATIAN COAST

WHY GO *Calm waters and a warm climate make this a perfect time to explore the gorgeous Dalmatian Coast. And what better way to experience the seascape than to hop from one idyllic island to another?*

The Dalmatian Coast has a treasure trove of delights—a glorious combination of historic towns, Roman ruins, Venetian palaces, miles and miles of coastline washed by crystal clear waters, and a warm, dry climate. And did we mention the islands? These are Croatia's jewels: the emerald, cypress-clad isles are set in an aquamarine sea and exquisitely finished with red-roofed towns. Follow the course of ancient explorers and negotiate the Adriatic Sea for yourself; there are a number of ferries between islands and the mainland, and private boats are available to rent.

As you hop from island to island—from Hvar to Split to Vis—you'll discover many spectacular spots to swim. The beaches are all pebbled, and those nearest to towns may be busy, but a little more effort will reward you with somewhere splendidly isolated. You'll find aromatic cypress and pine forests separated from the sea by a thin border of dark rocks—uncomfortably hot to start with, they make perfect diving platforms and, afterward, there's something wonderfully restorative about warming up on a toasty rock. If the heat gets too much, retire to the shade of the trees for a picnic lunch.

Speaking of food, there's little sustenance more satisfying than pizza and pasta. Italy may no longer lay claim to the region, but its cuisine has well and truly conquered it. And then there's Dalmatia's sumptuous seafood. What better way to experience the Dalmatian Coast than to island-hop, relaxing on each isle's beaches and gorging on its delicious cuisine?

When Else to Go

March–April Easter is a great time to visit, with locals giving brightly painted eggs as gifts. On Easter Day, eggs are hit against an opponent's; the one who emerges with an intact egg wins.

PLANNING YOUR TRIP **Getting there** The two main airports for Dalmatia are Dubrovnik Airport and Split Airport; both are about 12 miles (20 km) from their respective cities. Buses run from both airports into their city centers. **Getting around** You can rent your car at one airport and drop it off at the other. For getting around the islands, there are plenty of ferries, or rent your own boat. **Weather** June is a lovely time to visit, with pleasant temperatures. This is also one of the driest months. **Average temperature** 72°F / 22°C.

Two sailing boats gliding through the calm waters near a tiny and remote island off the Dalmatian Coast

KRUGER
NATIONAL PARK

A parade of elephants sauntering through grassland in Kruger National Park

Africa South Africa
KRUGER NATIONAL PARK

WHY GO *With fewer people and cooler temperatures, June is a great time for a safari in one of the world's most spectacular wildlife parks.*

Another day dawns on the plain, and animals begin to stir. On the grasslands around Satara, herds of zebras breakfast on the grass, tails swishing. A pair of giraffes, stooping as though conscious of their height, move off with surprising grace. A rhino can be heard crashing around in the woods. Suddenly, a pair of pricked ears, possibly belonging to a large cat, can just be seen in the savannah grass behind the zebra ... Kruger National Park has awoken.

With more varieties of animals than any other park in southern Africa, this is also one of the best places in the world to see the "Big Five." Its remarkable range of wildlife is explained by its huge variety of habitats. Amid the riverine woodland, short-sighted white rhinos lurk. North of the Olifants River, on the dry, dusty veldt, elephants amble. Along the plains south of the river, herds of zebras, giraffes, and antelopes sweep across the savannah. This is surely the best show on earth.

When Else to Go
February The weather is warmer, although the park does get busy with more safari expeditions.

PLANNING YOUR TRIP Getting there This park is around 310 miles (500 km) from Johannesburg, where most flights arrive into O R Tambo International Airport. Getting around The best way to travel is by car. Weather June is off-season and the weather is dry, sunny, and cool (it gets cold at night). Average temperature 63°F / 17°C.

THE BIG FIVE

1 Lions are undoubtedly one of the most magnificent sights in Kruger, and the park is home to one of the largest populations in Africa. You're most likely to glimpse or hear an adult lion at dawn or dusk.

2 Buffalo are the most numerous of the Big Five and travel in herds of 10 to 20 animals. They are powerfully built and unpredictable; they can be seen fighting off predatory lions—an incredible sight.

3 Rhinos—unlike the rest of the Big Five—are solitary animals. You're likely to spot a white rhino in the southern region of Kruger, where watering halls are evenly distributed.

4 Elephants are sociable creatures and travel in matriarchal clans—males leave the herd after 12 years. They communicate by subsonic rumbling, which travels through the earth.

5 Leopards are the most elusive of the Big Five. They are nocturnal, quiet, and fairly solitary. Leopards often climb trees *(below)* to escape danger and store their kills, so look up when you're exploring Kruger National Park.

// JULY

A fragrant lavender field
on a still summer
evening, Provence

MONGOLIA

Asia
MONGOLIA

WHY GO *The traditional festival of Naadam is held throughout Mongolia every summer, with the biggest event taking place in Ulaanbaatar.*

Situated at the foot of a range of hills, Ulaanbaatar is, above all, remote. While it may have many of the trappings of a modern city, its curious mix of Soviet-inspired architecture, remnants of its prerevolutionary history, and suburbs composed of neat rows of *gers* (traditional nomadic tents) lend it a charming air. However, getting into the countryside is the highlight of a visit to Mongolia. Most of this vast country is desert and grassland, and a major part of the population are still herdsmen of one kind or another, living as nomads.

At no time of year is this traditional lifestyle better seen than in mid-July, when the colorful Naadam Festival is held. For three days, this festival of games is celebrated. The country's greatest athletes compete in three classic Mongolian sports—horse racing, archery, and wrestling. On the Mongolian steppe, horse racing is a cross-country event, which takes place over vast open grasslands and follows no set course. Dressed in Genghis Khan warrior-style costumes, the men and women who compete in these tests of stamina and strength illustrate the warrior spirit that is still intrinsic to the Mongolian character.

When Else to Go
September During shoulder season, the weather is pleasantly cool.
October Bayan-Ölgii province hosts the Golden Eagle Festival.

PLANNING YOUR TRIP **Getting there** Flights arrive at Chinggis Khaan International Aiport, 11 miles (18 km) from Ulaanbaatar. **Getting around** Domestic flights and jeep transfers can be arranged. **Weather** Mongolia has short, warm summers. **Average temperature** 75°F / 24°C.

Mongolians on horseback racing across the Mongolian steppe during the Naadam Festival

WASHINGTON, D.C.

WASHINGTON, D.C.

WHY GO *This is party time in the US capital, and the National Mall, abuzz with a whole host of music, crafts, food, and entertainment, takes center stage.*

July sees the city at its vibrant best, with two of its most important events taking place in close succession. The first, the Smithsonian Folklife Festival, celebrates cultural heritage and is an entirely free, open-air event taking place in late June or early July. During the festival, the National Mall is filled with a colorful array of musicians, artists, story-tellers, cooks, and craftspeople, creating an energetic celebration. This is followed by Independence Day on the Fourth of July, when a real electricity descends on the city, as fireworks explode over the Washington Monument.

Even when the excitement of these festival days has died down, there is still much to be enchanted by, from a ride on a mule-drawn barge on the Chesapeake and Ohio Canal, to the National Museum of African American History and Culture, part of the world-leading Smithsonian Institution. There is nothing stuffy about this well-ordered, historic city—beneath its austere surface, you will find a very modern heart.

When Else to Go
March–April During the National Cherry Blossom Festival, the city celebrates the fragrant pink blooms that line the Mall.

PLANNING YOUR TRIP **Getting there** The city has three international airports: Dulles, Ronald Reagan Washington National Airport, and Baltimore-Washington. **Getting around** The metro and metrobuses are quick and cheap. **Weather** Hot and humid. **Average temperature** 88°F / 31°C.

Balloons flying around the US Capitol on the Fourth of July

Salzburg's old town overlooked by the forbidding Hohensalzburg Fortress

SALZBURG

Europe Austria
SALZBURG

WHY GO *During sonorous Salzburg's summer festival, city evenings take on a truly elegant air.*

Music is everywhere in Mozart's stylish, picturesque city of spires and domes, narrow streets, graceful squares, and pastel-painted facades. It rings out from carillons, fills the beautiful cathedral, and drifts through cobbled squares where talented young musicians play impromptu concertos. More than 4,000 cultural events take place in the city throughout the year, but the most coveted tickets are for the five-week Salzburg Festival, when packed concert halls, palaces, and churches resound to thrilling performances by some of the world's greatest performers. Images of the city and its surroundings never fail to beguile, but music remains at its soul.

When Else to Go
January The city celebrates the composer's birthday, on January 27, with Mozart Week—a series of concerts.

PLANNING YOUR TRIP **Getting there** From W. A. Mozart Airport, a bus goes to the railroad station and Mirabellplatz. **Getting around** The city is easily navigated on foot or by bike. **Weather** July is a warm month, with lots of sunshine and showers. **Average temperature** 81°F / 27°C.

PEMBROKESHIRE

Europe Wales
PEMBROKESHIRE

WHY GO *Once a land of warriors, southwest Wales is now for the adventurous. July is a lovely month to visit—the days are long, the land is lush, and the sea is cool and inviting.*

With its lush, green valleys and windswept mountains, Wales is rich in natural beauty, but the butter-soft beaches and ragged coastline of Pembrokeshire, in southwest Wales, are scene stealers. Here, dolphins frolic in the waves, seals sleep under craggy cliffs, and puffins spend their summer at Skomer Island—a rugged outcrop heaving with the little birds.

Framed by a 186-mile- (299-km-) long stretch of the Wales Coast Path, this is walking country. The landscape changes with every step as you traverse steep limestone cliffs, follow golden beaches, and navigate glacial valleys. Hop from B&B to B&B, staying in cabins, family homes, and shepherd's huts. Famously friendly, your hosts will likely drive any luggage on to your next stop so that it doesn't hinder your walk.

Want to get the adrenaline pumping? Don a helmet and life jacket, find a guide, and try your hand at coasteering. This extreme rock pooling will see you exploring caves and jumping into waves. If you'd rather leave it to the professionals, Abereiddi's Blue Lagoon has hosted many editions of the Red Bull Cliff Diving World Series. And the Irish Sea offers wave riders everything from bodyboarding to surfing.

When you've worked up an appetite, chow down on tender local lamb, in a gastropub, order the catch-of-the-day at a "chippy," or try laverbread—the "Welshman's caviar."

When Else to Go
September–November In fall, fluffy gray seal pups lounge around in Pembrokeshire's pebbled coves.

Above Ragged coast-line near St. Davids, Pembrokeshire

Right Walking along the Pembrokeshire Coast Path; resident puffins

PLANNING YOUR TRIP **Getting there** Cardiff is two hours by train from central London. Take the train, or drive, from there to the southwest coast. **Getting around** Five coastal bus services traverse the length of Pembrokeshire. **Weather** Days are usually warm, but be prepared for some rain. **Average temperature** 68°F / 20°C.

A gorgeous sunset over
Porthgain Harbour,
Pembrokeshire

CORSICA

Europe France
CORSICA

WHY GO *A summer playground, this island's astonishing landscape serves as the perfect backdrop for a huge range of exciting activities.*

A landscape shrouded in myth, Corsica is a place of mysterious beauty. This is a craggy, wild land, its interior peppered with peaks. Once believed to have been the home of giants and ogres, the fourth largest island in the Mediterranean is now a popular summer hot spot. And it's no surprise: it combines sunshine with charming, small towns; lush, green forests; cool, clear rivers; and soft, white-sand beaches from which you can let the days drift past.

But Corsica isn't a stage set—it invites exploration. Take a horse ride through the green hills of the Castagniccia or along the sandy shores of the lovely east coast, or rent bicycles and find the perfect picnic spot. Many of Corsica's rivers are quite spectacular, ideal for canoeing or an exhilarating rafting expedition. The many footpaths are perfect for discovering some of the island's 2,000 species of flora.

When you've had your fill of activities and just want to laze in the sun and splash around in the sea, you again have lots of choices. Seek out the magnificent coves in the south, such as

The sun rising over Corsica's rugged Aiguilles de Bavella

Rondinara Bay, where fine, white sand leads down to unbelievably clear water, or take a boat to virtually inaccessible Saleccia Beach in the north. This island really does pack a punch.

When Else to Go

May–June Early summer is a quieter time to visit the island, plus the weather is still bound to be lovely—if a little less hot than in July.

PLANNING YOUR TRIP **Getting there** Corsica has four airports: Ajaccio, Bastia, Calvi, and Figari. **Getting around** Renting a car is the easiest way to get around. **Weather** Generally hot and dry, but cooler in the mountains. **Average temperature** 86°F / 30°C.

CORSICA IN BLOOM

In May, hundreds of native wildflowers color the island's *maquis* (scrubland) and fill the air with their sweet aroma.

Fenouil One of the strongest scents of the *maquis* comes from the bright yellow blooms of wild fennel, which is often used to flavor local dishes.

Myrtle This small tree is a symbol of love and immortality. It's dark-blue berries are used to make the famous *licòr di mortula*. It is also a staple of Corsican cuisine.

Sweet Broom In late spring and early summer, broom covers the hillsides in dramatic yellow swaths and delicate perfume.

BERLIN

Europe Germany
BERLIN

WHY GO *Berlin is awash with the colors of the rainbow flag in July as Pride events are held throughout the city, culminating in one of Europe's biggest and brightest street parties and parades.*

Berlin has been a center of LGBTQ+ life in Germany since the early Weimar years. This combined with the city's reputation for wild parties means its annual Pride festival is one of the best in Europe, and July is packed with events—everything from drag nights to film screenings. The jewel in its crown is the Pride parade, held at the end of the month and often drawing 500,000 participants. It's a great opportunity to experience Berliners' creativity, exuberance, and welcoming spirit, whether you're a member of the LGBTQ+ community or an ally.

The parade begins at Kurfürstendamm, where trucks and buses play pounding music, each vying playfully with the next to attract a bigger crowd.

And what a crowd—in an event focused on inclusivity and acceptance, it's no surprise that the participants are a varied bunch. From jeans and T-shirts to full drag and rainbow bodysuits, every style of clothing is welcome. At noon, the parade starts, dancing its way down the city's broad avenues and past historic buildings, finally reaching the Brandenburg Gate where there's a rousing rally.

Once the official event is over, it's time to party in clubs and bars across the city. By the time you're weaving your way home, the parade route will have been cleaned up, but the remaining specks of glitter left between the cobblestones will serve as a reminder that the city's Weimar-era dreams are alive and well.

When Else to Go
May The bitter cold of winter has dissipated and open-air events across the city begin in earnest.

PLANNING YOUR TRIP **Getting there** Flights arrive into Tegel Airport, 7 miles (12 km) northwest of Berlin, and Schönefeld, 11 miles (18 km) southeast of the city. Both are easily accessible by public transportation. Berlin Brandenburg is also under construction; the opening is scheduled for 2020, after which Tegel may close. **Getting around** The public transportation system is made up of the U-Bahn and S-Bahn, buses, and trams. **Weather** Warm and sunny, with occasional showers. **Average temperature** 73°F / 23°C.

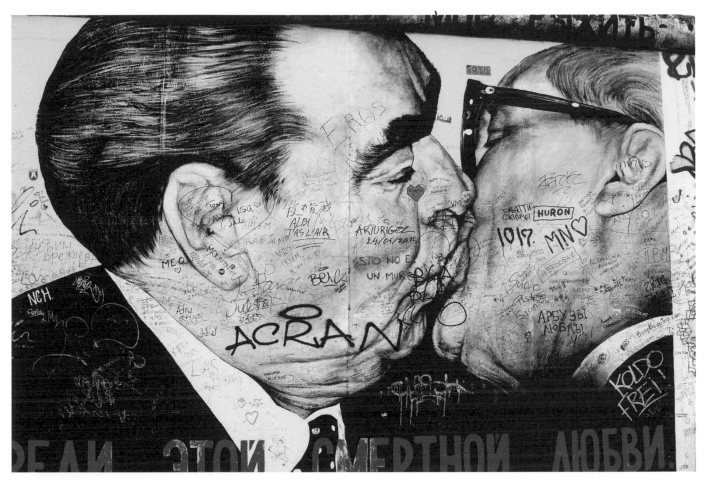

Clockwise from top *My God, Help Me to Survive This Deadly Love* by Dmitri Vrubel, a mural on the Berlin Wall; a rainbow flag waving in front of the landmark Berlin TV Tower; a Pride participant wearing elaborate makeup

Europe Norway
SVALBARD

WHY GO *Norway's glacial outpost enjoys the 24-hour sunshine of the Arctic summer. The archipelago is home to stunning wildlife, including polar bears, which you're most likely to see in July.*

Bathed in the perpetual sunlight of midsummer, Svalbard in July presents an unrivaled glimpse of the polar north. After most of the pack ice has retreated and snow has melted in low-lying areas, boats arrive in their dozens, migrating birds return to nest on towering sea cliffs, and wildflowers emerge to splash color across the lonely, treeless tundra of this Arctic archipelago.

The Svalbard experience begins in the town of Longyearbyen, which nestles near the foot of two glaciers at the mouth of Adventdalen Valley. Perhaps because the sun is visible around the clock from mid-April to October, the tempo of life is upbeat in the summer, with locals partying into the early hours. Just outside of town, however, the wilderness begins, inspiring a real sense of adventure and discovery. The biting wind carries the cries of sea birds—puffins, guillemots, cormorants, gulls, and others—that occupy cliff-hugging nests, rearing the season's chicks. Along tame shorelines, it's a joy to wander over the landscape in search of wild-flowers and the rusting remnants of adventurers past. There's a chance of spotting a reindeer or a wandering Arctic fox, but surely no wildlife experience compares with the thrill of seeing a polar bear lumbering across the icy tundra, and, given that there are more polar bears than people here, it is not such an unlikely sight.

When Else to Go
September The last chance to see polar bears before the archipelago freezes over.

PLANNING YOUR TRIP
Getting there Svalbard Airport is in Longyearbyen, with flights arriving from Tromsø, 600 miles (1,000 km) south. **Getting around** An organized tour or cruise is recommended, or you can rent a car. **Weather** July is mostly dry but cold, with bracing winds. **Average temperature** 41°F / 5°C.

"Just outside of town, however, the wilderness begins, inspiring a real sense of adventure and discovery."

Clockwise from top left
A polar bear and her cubs crossing pack ice in Spitsbergen, north-west of Longyearbyen; summer meltwater forming a waterfall on an ice cap in Svalbard; a lone reindeer standing on grassland

PROVENCE

Europe France
PROVENCE

WHY GO *During the height of summer, the landscape is peppered with fields of purple lavender, and the air is heavy with its sweet perfume.*

Vast sunflower prairies and violet-hued lavender fields are illuminated in the summer sun, their regimented rows fading to a distant horizon. This is quintessential Provence. July may be the busiest month to visit this most dazzling corner of France, but it is also the most magical. Throughout the summer, whole hillsides are awash with glorious shades of deep purple, plum, and blue-violet. For the classic view, head to the Abbaye Notre-Dame de Sénanque, where blossoms create a bee-buzzing haze of color, scent, and sound around the ancient cloisters. The Valensole Plateau is another favorite, where numerous sunflower and lavender fields are easily reachable by car.

When Else to Go
September As summer crowds start to dwindle, the grape harvest season begins.

PLANNING YOUR TRIP **Getting there** The main airports are Marseille Provence and Nice Côte d'Azur. **Getting around** The coast is served by reliable bus and train networks. **Weather** Hot and dry. **Average temperature** 75°F / 24°C.

Seemingly endless rows of purple lavender in full bloom on the Valensole Plateau

Right Enjoying a ride at Tivoli on a summer evening

Below Bikes and barges lining Nyhavn, Copenhagen's most iconic canal

COPENHAGEN

Europe Denmark
COPENHAGEN

WHY GO *Famously cool Copenhagen is abuzz in July, with locals flocking to the pretty canals and sprawling parks that pepper the Danish capital. There are plenty of summer events to keep you entertained, including a number of music festivals.*

Throngs of cyclists expertly navigate the city's streets and bridges, pausing to chat and enjoy a cup of coffee. The city's numerous parks are sprinkled with Copenhageners enjoying picnics, walking their dogs, playing frisbee, and generally indulging in the Danish art of *hygge*. Photogenic waterways lined with veteran barges thrum with locals and visitors rubbing shoulders as they eat, drink, and put the world to rights, and—in the designated swimming zones—the sounds of splashing and infectious laughter ring out. Welcome to wonderful Copenhagen.

A trip to Copenhagen wouldn't be complete without a visit to Tivoli, an amusement park with more rides than you can fit into a day—from simple carousels to twisting roller coasters, plus concerts, restaurants, and beautiful gardens that are bursting with blooms in July. At dusk, 100,000 soft-glow lights turn Tivoli into an enchanting fairyland.

This utterly magical city, with its medieval cobbled streets and trendy neighborhoods, also welcomes a plethora of music festivals in July. With the Copenhagen Opera Festival, Roskilde Festival, and Copenhagen Jazz Festival, music fills the streets until the late hours. Draw up a chair, grab a drink, sit back, and enjoy.

When Else to Go
October Halloween at Tivoli and fall colors throughout the city.

PLANNING YOUR TRIP **Getting there** Copenhagen has excellent connections by air, rail, road, and sea. Frequent trains shuttle from Kastrup Airport to the city center in 15 minutes. **Getting around** There's a superb public transportation system of buses, metro, waterbuses, trains, and city bikes. **Weather** July is usually the sunniest month, with long and mild days. **Average temperature** 72°F / 22°C.

// AUGUST

Steam rising from Castle
Geyser in Yellowstone
National Park

BOROBUDUR

Asia Indonesia
BOROBUDUR

WHY GO *With the rains long finished, the skies are mercifully clear, providing the perfect backdrop to this sublime monument.*

Traveling through the lush plantations and terraced rice fields of central Java, you don't see Borobudur until you arrive at the gateway to the monument. Then, through the flame trees and palm groves, it suddenly materializes.

One of the world's largest religious monuments, with nine levels, towers, niches, and countless stupas, Borobudur's power lies in its five levels of sublime carvings. Be prepared for a long walk as you examine the images at the lower levels, which depict daily life in the 8th century and, farther up, dedications to the life of the Buddha. At the upper levels, the smaller stupas contain meditating Buddhas, but, at the top, the central stupa is mysteriously empty, suggesting nirvana, the ultimate state of nothingness. Emerging from this, with just the sky above you and the plains stretching out below toward the awesome Merapi volcano, the most active on earth, you will suddenly feel liberated. The serenity may be short-lived—this is the country's most popular site— but, as you return through the tropical countryside, you cannot help but feel that you've had a vision of the divine.

When Else to Go
October The rainy season is yet to begin but already the surrounding countryside appears green and lush.

The majestic Borobudur, an 8th–9th-century Buddhist temple, at sunset

PLANNING YOUR TRIP Getting there International flights arrive at Jakarta, which is linked to Yogyakarta and Solo airports. **Getting around** Arrange a tour from Yogyakarta. **Weather** Warm and humid. **Average temperature** 80°F / 27°C.

LUCERNE

Europe Switzerland
LUCERNE

WHY GO *Coincide your visit to this enchanting medieval city with its international classical music festival.*

Surrounded by mountains on the western shore of the lake that shares its name, there can be few festival towns that enjoy Lucerne's idyllic setting. The city's reputation as a leading classical and contemporary music hub is well established, and its annual festival, an impressive display of symphony concerts, galas, and opera, attracts music fans in their thousands.

Should it set in, festival fatigue can easily be dispersed by a trip to the mountains. Reach the top via the world's steepest cogwheel railroad and gasp at the panorama before you—flower-carpeted meadows leading down to the lakeside town, where, as dusk falls, myriad lights begin to twinkle.

When Else to Go
February/March Join the locals as they don masks and costumes for a few days of merriment and music during *fasnacht*.

PLANNING YOUR TRIP **Getting there**
Arrive into Zürich then travel by car or train.
Getting around Lucerne is best explored on foot.
Weather Warm with occasional cloudy days.
Average temperature 77°F / 25°C.

The picturesque wooden Chapel Bridge, crossing over the sheer waters of Lucerne's Reuss River

Europe Germany
BLACK FOREST

WHY GO *August is the perfect time to visit the Black Forest as the days are long, warm, and sunny—great for getting out and about in the hills and mountains.*

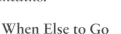

BLACK FOREST

If you ever wanted to see the archetypal fairy-tale forest, visit the Schwarzwald (Black Forest). Here, you'll discover dreamy country-side with rolling hills, mountainous ridges, and deep river gorges; crystal clear lakes, perfect for a cooling dip; and welcoming villages.

The area is a paradise for outdoor enthusiasts who want a great adventure, and, of course, there are hundreds of miles of well-marked hiking paths. Many follow century-old trails, forging a path through wooded valleys, past charming villages and glacier lakes. If you make it into the mountains, the Black Forest is also famous for its hot springs and healthy waters. Here, you can relax in a steam sauna or simply float in a hot tub, drifting away into your own fairy tale.

When Else to Go
July Hot, sultry days transform into incredible thunder storms, which make for dramatic photographs. **December** Christmas markets spring up in nearly every town in the region.

PLANNING YOUR TRIP **Getting there** Fly into Frankfurt, then travel on to Baden-Baden, near the Black Forest. **Getting around** Use Germany's excellent trains or rent a car. **Weather** Sunny and mild days. **Average temperature** 68°F / 20°C.

Morning mist settling over the Black Forest

MANU NATIONAL PARK

South America Peru
MANU NATIONAL PARK

WHY GO *Described as the most biodiverse protected area on the planet, Manu National Park is ripe for exploration. Come during the dry season to ensure access to hiking trails.*

Manu National Park is the largest tropical park in South America and home to an extraordinary diversity of plants and wildlife. Found in this jungle are more than 850 species of birds, including the cock-of-the-rock, 200 species of mammals, such as the majestic jaguar, and more than 15,000 species of plants. All of this is remarkably preserved due to the inaccessibility of the area and monitoring of visitor numbers. No commercial activity is permitted here, and tourists are not allowed to stay overnight in the park, so you'll stay in a rustic lodge (limited or no electricity and accessible only by boat), located just outside.

Hiking along forested trails in search of tapir and the elusive jaguar brings out the adventurer in visitors. On the river, the boat becomes silent as everyone waits with bated breath for the slick head of a rare giant otter to emerge from the water or for a black cayman to catch the light as it slides into the mud. Plowing deeper into the reserve aboard a motor-canoe, the foliage becomes thicker, the humidity more intense, and the chattering of monkeys and birds and the steady hum of insects almost deafening. The scale of the jungle is breathtaking. For sheer wilderness, it doesn't get much better than this.

When Else to Go
November Come at the start of the rainy season to see more amphibians.

PLANNING YOUR TRIP **Getting there** Fly into Lima and then on to Cusco. A further short flight on a small twin-engined plane will get you to Boca Manú. A motorized canoe takes you on the 90-minute trip down the Madre de Dios River to your accommodations. **Getting around** In the park, all your trips, on land or water, will be with a guide. **Weather** The dry season can be quite humid. **Average temperature** 64–88°F / 18–31°C.

"The boat becomes silent as everyone waits with bated breath for the slick head of a rare giant otter to emerge from the water."

Above The lush, green mountains of Manu

Left A kaleidoscope of macaws on a clay lick; the elusive jaguar

YELLOWSTONE
NATIONAL PARK

YELLOWSTONE NATIONAL PARK

WHY GO *August brings the best weather, and while this is a popular time for visitors, you can avoid the bulk of the crowds if you stray from the beaten path.*

More than half a million years ago, a gargantuan volcanic explosion blanketed western North America in ash and scooped out a vast caldera 45 miles by 30 miles (72 km by 50 km) wide. Today that caldera, located just north of the spectacular Grand Teton Mountains, is green and lush with meadows and an incredible diversity of wildlife. Stunning tableaus of wild rivers, azure lakes, and snowcapped peaks set the backdrop for an otherworldly landscape of steaming fumaroles, geysers, bubbling mud pots, and psychedelically colored thermal springs. This is Yellowstone National Park.

Though August is a busy time, discovering the real wilderness beauty of Yellowstone is as simple as getting off the beaten path anywhere in the park. Crisscrossing the grassy flats and mountain plateaus, pine forests, and limestone terraces is a 1,300-mile (2,000-km-) trail system, providing plenty of opportunity to find solitude. A walk along the South Rim Trail east from busy Artist Point leads you up a brief, steep ascent that takes you far from the crowds. Following the gentle terrain of the canyon rim, the trail offers stunning views of the canyon, the Yellowstone River, and the cascading cataract of lower falls that are as visually captivating as they were when the park was first discovered.

When Else to Go

May Avoid the crowds and visit the park as it's opening up again. This is a great time for wildlife, too: look out for bison calves and bear cubs.

PLANNING YOUR TRIP Getting there The closest major international airport to Yellowstone National Park is in Salt Lake City, Utah; alternatively, fly into regional airports in Wyoming, Montana, or Idaho. **Getting around** Rent a car in Salt Lake City for the 320-mile (515-km) drive to Yellowstone. **Weather** August days are long and warm. Thunderstorms are frequent. **Average temperature** 86°F / 30°C.

HIKES AROUND THE PARK

1 Old Faithful is the park's most famous geyser, but there are more to see. Follow the **Norris Geyser Basin Trail** through this geothermal hot spot to discover rare, acid ones like Echinus Geyser.

2 See bison, grizzly bears, and elk from the **Hayden Valley Trail**, between Yellowstone Lake and the Grand Canyon of Yellowstone.

3 Family-favorite **Trout Lake Loop** is great for wildlife spotting. See otters frolicking in the water during the summer months.

4 There are hikes for all levels around the rim of the Grand Canyon of the Yellowstone. The **Artist Point Trail** leads to particularly lovely views of the canyon and Lower Yellowstone Falls.

5 The strenuous **Avalanche Peak Trail** takes you to superb views of the park's tallest peaks. July and August is the sweet spot between snowfall and grizzly season.

TOP TIP

There is a wealth of information at the park's visitors' centers. Pick up park maps and brochures, get the latest updates on wildlife viewing, and peruse well-curated exhibits on Yellowstone's history, geology, and wildlife.

"Stunning tableaus of wild rivers, azure lakes, and snow-capped peaks set the backdrop for an otherworldly landscape."

Clockwise from top An aerial view of the Grand Prismatic Spring; the Mammoth Hot Springs; bison grazing the prairie below the Grand Teton Mountains

Kayaking on icy
waters in the epic
Glacier Bay
National Park,
surrounded by
mountain scenery

GLACIER BAY
NATIONAL PARK

North America US
GLACIER BAY NATIONAL PARK

WHY GO *Whale-watching opportunities are at a high during summer, as whales return to Alaska's waters after spending the winter in warmer climes.*

Little compares to seeing a house-sized block of ice crashing into the water or a huge humpback whale seemingly defying gravity as it breaks the surface, but these scenes are common in Alaska's Glacier Bay.

In this ever-changing landscape of impressive glaciers, snowcapped mountains, and icy waters, there is abundant wildlife. On a good day, you might see the spouting and splashing of breaching whales, hear the cries of sea birds, watch comical sea otters play and bald eagles wheel overhead, and perhaps even see a brown bear methodically plodding along the shore. But the real thrill is in watching a massive block of ice dislodge from the glacier face and slide silently into the sea. A second or two later comes the thunderous crack of the breaking ice, followed by a lineup of swells that cause your boat to bob up and down like a cork. This is nature at its most sublime.

When Else to Go
April Combine a visit to Glacier Bay with the annual Alaska Folk Festival, held in Juneau, for a week of concerts and dances.

PLANNING YOUR TRIP **Getting there** Fly from Juneau International Airport to Gustavus, 10 miles (16 km) from the park headquarters at Bartlett Cove. There are also ferries, but many visitors arrive by cruise ship. **Getting around** The bay is best seen aboard cruise ships, tour boats, and kayaks. **Weather** Cool and often rainy, with some sunny periods. **Average temperature** 57°F / 14°C.

KANDY

ELLA

Asia Sri Lanka
KANDY TO ELLA

WHY GO *The "Tea Train" from Kandy to Ella serves up a seductive blend of spectacular scenery and Sri Lankan sociability. The rains have eased, too, so the view from your train car is totally unspoiled.*

There are few things that withstand a "world's most beautiful" moniker, but the train journey that runs through Sri Lanka's Hill Country pulls it off. This is a region of mist-shrouded mountains; rolling hillsides carpeted with lush, green tea plantations; and rushing waterfalls—and there's no better way to see it than from the window of a train.

Built to transport tea from the hills to the country's capital, Colombo, the railroads snaking through the region have become a hit with travelers. The route from Kandy to Ella takes around seven hours, but the most memorable section is the four hours from Hatton to Ella, at the highest point of the line. As the train grinds patiently upward, increasingly majestic views over the craggy green hills are revealed. Tea is everywhere—a seemingly endless swath of bright green bushes creeping up impossible gradients, speckled with the tiny figures of Tamil tea pickers hunched over the bushes. As the train winds its way through valleys, there are glimpses of dozens of waterfalls cascading down cliff faces, while from cliff edges, mist and cloud transforms the landscape into a mysterious milky blur.

Regular stops at a series of quaint, toylike stations, complete with their original hand-painted signs and colonial-era fixtures, punctuate the journey. Train cars are visited by roving hawkers waving bunches of bananas and freshly fried piles of samosas, before a deafening blast of the horn signals departure time, and the train rolls slowly onward again.

When Else to Go
April The Hill Country is alive as the locals celebrate the Sinhalese–Tamil New Year with ten days of festivities.

PLANNING YOUR TRIP **Getting there** Fly into Colombo International Airport **Getting around** From Colombo, board the train to Kandy then on to Ella. Tickets go on sale 30 days in advance; book early. **Weather** Warm with regular showers; evenings are cool. **Average temperature** 77°F / 25°C.

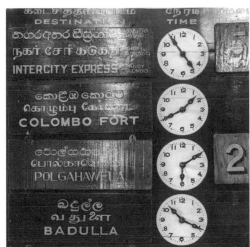

Right Picking tea in the Hill Country; train timetable at Kandy station

Below Enjoying the view aboard the "Tea Train" from Kandy to Ella

The beautiful Lake Bled, surrounded by the soaring peaks of the Julian Alps, perfect for an outdoor adventure

SLOVENIA

Europe
SLOVENIA

WHY GO *Make the most of long, warm days during Slovenia's summer and plan an active trip in the country's scenic settings.*

Blessed with voluminous snow-capped mountain peaks, sparkling lakes, gushing waterfalls, and glacial valleys, Slovenia is packed with picture-perfect views. One of the most iconic images of the country is the ethereal Lake Bled, lauded by local poet France Prešeren as "this second Eden, full of charm and grace." Admiring its mist-shrouded island church, which reclines under the protective eye of Bled Castle and the vaulting mountain peaks of the Julian Alps, it's hard to disagree.

The true joy in a visit to Slovenia, however, is getting out and about in its unspoiled countryside. This is truly an outdoor destination, with hiking, trekking, mountain biking, caving, and canyoning all offered. In Triglav, the country's only national park, hiking 9,400 ft (2,864 m) to the summit of the park's eponymous mountain is something of a rite of passage for Slovenes—so why not join them? In nearby Bohinj, there is even more unspoiled countryside ripe for exploration and Slovenia's largest lake, the glacial Lake Bohinj. This stunning expanse of alpine water is framed by the hulking mountains, with picturesque lake cruises and a range of outdoor sports like paragliding, kayaking, and horse riding available during the long summer days.

South of the Julian Alps in the Soča Valley, a water wonderland awaits, where, amid rugged mountain peaks and leafy forest, the brilliant emerald-colored Soča River attracts whitewater rafters from all over Europe. If a white-knuckle ride on the river isn't for you, then try a canoe or mountain bike trip instead. Whatever you go for, you're guaranteed a memorable alpine adventure.

When Else to Go

October Visit to see the spectacular fall colors and make the most of the harvest season on a wine-tasting tour.

PLANNING YOUR TRIP Getting there International flights arrive in the capital, Ljubljana. **Getting around** An efficient bus network links most places to Ljubljana, but rail services are more limited. Renting a car is recommended. **Weather** Days are pleasantly warm, but it can get a lot colder at higher altitudes. **Average temperature** 77°F / 25°C.

WILD SWIMMING SPOTS

Slovenia's crystal clear lakes, glittering rivers, and spectacular waterfalls make this an ideal location for a refreshing dip.

The blue-green **Lake Bled** is the most iconic of Slovenia's lakes. The designated swimming area is near the magnificent castle rock.

Just 9 miles (15 km) south of Ljubljana, **Podpeško Lake** is the locals' choice. It also happens to be the deepest lake in Slovenia.

Lake Jasna comprises two small artificial lakes. Set against a backdrop of jagged mountain peaks, the view from this alpine lake is nothing short of breathtaking.

MOZAMBIQUE

Right Snorkeling through a coral reef; a humpback whale off the coast; three bottlenose dolphins

Below Azure waters and golden sands in the Bazaruto Archipelago

Africa
MOZAMBIQUE

WHY GO *Visit Mozambique in August to see migrating humpback whales and frolicking dolphins.*

Long one of Southern Africa's least-known destinations, Mozambique is rapidly gaining a reputation as a diving mecca. Its magnificent coastline, more than 1,240 miles (2,000 km) long and speckled with islands, is home to myriad marine life and little-explored coral reefs perfect for an underwater adventure.

A highlight is the Bazaruto Archipelago. Seen from above, brilliant turquoises, aquas, and deep blues swirl together with green and jade tones, all in stunning contrast to the shimmering white sand banks and beaches. In the water, humpback whales and dolphins share the sea with an impressive array of beautiful tropical fish. Still a little-visited jewel on a vast continent, Mozambique's many treasures truly are spectacular.

When Else to Go
September The dry season continues providing plenty of opportunity for a beach vacation.

PLANNING YOUR TRIP **Getting there** Fly into Johannesburg, then on to Maputo, Mozambique's capital. **Getting around** From Maputo, internal flights connect to the Bazaruto Archipelago. **Weather** Sunny, dry, and warm. **Average temperature** 75°F / 24°C.

// SEPTEMBER

Ballooning over the sweeping ochre dunes of Namibia's Namib-Naukluft Park

Europe Germany
MUNICH

WHY GO *Join the locals for Oktoberfest, the world's biggest beer festival, a boisterous yet charming celebration of German* Gemütlichkeit *(sociability), with beer,* Brez'n *(pretzels), and partying.*

Despite its name, Oktoberfest usually starts in September, under the fall sun. Over the course of 16 days, Munich moves to the joyous sounds of oompah bands, clinking steins, and a constant chorus of *"prost!"* (cheers). More than 6 million dirndl- and lederhosen-clad visitors descend on the city every year to drink some 10.5 million pints (60,000 hectoliters) of beer. The favorite tents enjoy such incredible hype that reservations are necessary. But what do you expect at an uber party like this?

When Else to Go
December Marienplatz, the city's central square, hosts one of Germany's prettiest Christmas markets.

PLANNING YOUR TRIP **Getting there** Munich International Airport is well connected. **Getting around** Explore the center on foot. **Weather** Sunny and dry. **Average temperature** 60°F / 16°C.

Freshly shucked oysters garnished with lemons

Revelers drinking steins of beer in one of Oktoberfest's most popular tents

Europe Ireland
GALWAY

GALWAY

WHY GO *Wash oysters down with pints of the "black stuff" during this foodie festival that hits the city of Galway at the end of September.*

During the four-day Galway International Oyster and Seafood Festival, the emphasis rests on fun, food, and, of course, filling up with Guinness—the national drink. The main attraction of the festivities is the oysters, which are carefully selected from beds within the pure waters of Galway Bay, where the native oyster still grows wild.

On Saturday afternoon, the "cracking" Guinness World Oyster Opening Championships starts off the proceedings, with eager competitors frantically trying to beat the shucking world record. For the next three days, festivalgoers can sample these succulent, salty oysters in the festival marquee, while they listen to buoyant live music or watch one of the nation's hottest chefs demonstrate how to prepare the decadent shellfish for themselves.

If oysters aren't for you, don't despair. The festival runs a program of foodie-oriented talks on a variety of subjects, and some of Galway's best restaurants host tasting events to coincide with the festival. Don't miss, too, the Mardi Gras–style Gala Event, when the walk past the Spanish Arch to Nimmo's Pier—where the marquee is erected—takes you through a sea of high heels and *haute couture*. Whether you're drinking, dancing, or devouring oysters, there is always more than enough *craic* to go around.

When Else to Go

July Ireland is at its warmest at the height of summer, and the Galway International Arts Festival brings actors, musicians, and artists to the city.

PLANNING YOUR TRIP **Getting there** Galway Airport is 6 miles (10 km) from the city center and is accessible by internal fights from Dublin Airport. **Getting around** There are taxis and buses, but the center is easily covered on foot. **Weather** Generally mild, but rain is not unusual. **Average temperature** 54°F / 12°C.

NAMIB-NAUKLUFT PARK

Africa Namibia
NAMIB-NAUKLUFT PARK

WHY GO *At the height of the dry season, Namibia's wildlife congregate around rare rivers and oasis-like waterholes. This makes September one of the best times to visit this lunar landscape.*

Namibia must rank close to being the emptiest nonpolar nation on the planet. Dominated by the Namib Desert, whose parched, sandy soils are teased by less than 1 inch (2.5 cm) of rain annually, this immense land is too desiccated to sit comfortably with adjectives such as pretty or beautiful. Yet there is a vastness to the Namibian landscape, a ravaged majesty that is at once humbling and breathtaking.

The 19,000-sq-mile (50,000-sq-km) Namib-Naukluft—one of Africa's largest national parks—is home to Sossusvlei. Here, you'll find the world's tallest dunes: rippled apricot mountains whose curvaceous "scorpion tails" tower above a series of seasonal pans that fill with water once or perhaps twice in a decade. Here, too, is the aptly named Deadvlei, its embalmed floor of cracked mud hosting a spectral forest, a relic of the days when this parody of a lake received water more regularly.

Come dusk, you might see a herd of oryx antelope filing regally across a dune crest, a meerkat family standing to attention in the dying light, or a spiky quiver tree silhouetted against the disappearing sun. The crisp, clear desert air and absence of competing light sources make the Namib night sky a thing of shimmering, awe-inspiring beauty. No less memorable is the silence of the desert on a windless night—so close to absolute that it becomes almost tangible, an enveloping presence broken sporadically by the gentle chatter of a gecko or the demented whooping of a distant hyena or jackal.

When Else to Go

March–April Featuring a parade, music performances, and a masked ball, Windhoek Karneval (WIKA) is the premier event in Namibia's calendar. Its origins lie in the country's time as a German colony.

The skeleton of a dead tree silhouetted against the white clay pan of Deadvlei

PLANNING YOUR TRIP **Getting there** Namibia's international airport, Hosea Kutako, is 28 miles (46 km) from the capital, Windhoek. **Getting around** A car is essential, even within the National Park. To the north, the cities of Windhoek and Swakopmund are connected by roads, as well as daily flights. **Weather** Dry and pleasantly warm. Cold at night and in the morning. **Average temperature** 77°F / 25°C.

VERMONT

North America US
NORTHEAST VERMONT

WHY GO *The flaming hues of Vermont's fall foliage are an annual spectacle. Enjoy the colors without the crowds in the state's rugged and remote "Northeast Kingdom."*

With its bucolic mountains and rolling hills, Vermont is arguably one of the most scenic corners of America, blessed with an abundance of sugar maple trees that not only produce the Green Mountain State's famous maple syrup but are responsible for the distinctive bright red leaves that make this one of fall's most colorful destinations.

Leaf peepers look no further. A scenic drive through Vermont's unspoiled rural northeast, known simply as the "Kingdom" to understandably empassioned locals, will reveal Norway maples ablaze in scarlet and orange; sugar maples in cardinal red; and birches, beeches, and alders aglow in luminous yellow. This is where the spectacle of the changing seasons is at its most dramatic. But Northeast Vermont offers so much more than great views from behind

the wheel. Here, you'll find farm stands filled to the brim with freshly harvested goodies, inviting restaurants that celebrate farm-to-fork produce, quaint country stores, and charming inns, not to mention the many eclectic museums and antique stores.

A particular highlight is the annual Northeast Kingdom Foliage Festival, which rotates from town to town for a week during late September and early October. Each town hosts its own day and offers all manner of exciting activities, from guided ghost walks through the pretty town of Peacham to artisan cheese tasting in Cabot, all set against a beautiful backdrop of vibrant fall color.

When Else to Go
February Hit the slopes when ski season is in full swing.

Above A spectacular display of color on the banks of Long Pond, Greensboro

Right Freshly harvested sweet corn; walking through the woodland in Vermont; fall colors in Peacham

---

PLANNING YOUR TRIP **Getting there** Vermont's major airport is in Burlington, 77 miles (124 km) from St. Johnsbury. More international flights arrive into Boston, 150 miles (240 km) away. **Getting around** Renting a car is the best way to tour this leafy corner of New England. **Weather** Mild but changeable. **Average temperature** 64°F / 18°C.

A traditional wooden *gulet* in a secluded Lycian bay in south-western Turkey

LYCIAN COAST

Europe Turkey
LYCIAN COAST

WHY GO *As summer fades, the sea is still at its warmest—perfect timing for a peaceful cruise around the rugged cliffs and shingle bays of Turkey's spectacular Lycian coast.*

Southwestern Turkey is home to more ancient ruins area-for-area than any other region in the world. Since time immemorial, conquerors, traders, and travelers have beaten a path to these mighty monuments, set spectacularly on the crumbling hillsides, yet the sites still never fail to impress. Majestic and serene, they loom over everything, colonized only by the wildflowers and butterflies that make their homes here. And what better way to see them than from a *gulet*, a traditional Turkish wooden sailboat.

Sail smoothly past these wonders and pine-forested hillsides, as the sunlight dances on the surface of the turquoise sea, and you enjoy a meal of fresh fish cooked on board. Stop occasionally for a refreshing swim or to moor in a pretty little town. Around another spit of land, a sheltered cove or beautiful beach beckons from the foot of a towering cliff. The Mediterranean, set against the bleached blocks of old stone, looks almost luminous in its blueness as a couple of other *gulets* slowly drift by, shimmering and hazy in the heavy heat of the afternoon sun.

As the daylight begins to fade, tour groups vanish, and the ruins are deserted once again. Highlighted against a darkening sky, the scenery seems as timeless and enduring today as it must have done millennia ago.

When Else to Go
April The weather is equally pleasant, and colorful spring flowers pepper the hillsides.

PLANNING YOUR TRIP Getting there International airports include Antalya, Bodrum, Dalaman, and Izmir. **Getting around** *Gulet* (traditional Turkish boat) cruises can be booked in advance privately or as part of a group. **Weather** September has warm, sunny days. **Average temperature** 75°F / 24°C.

ANCIENT SITES

Ancient Lycia once comprised 19 mountain cities. The ruins and antiquities of these strongholds are today stunning places to explore.

Myra *(above)* was an ancient Greek city, where citizens worshipped the goddess Artemis. The acropolis, baths, and amphitheater are all staggeringly beautiful; look for the carved mask reliefs in the theater.

Pinara has a sense of mystery and makes for lovely exploration, with the scent of pines clinging to the air. The amphitheater at the base of the ancient city is impressive, as are the tombs that pockmark the mountain sides.

Letoon was an ancient Greek sanctuary, where Leto and her children, Apollo and Artemis, were worshipped. Strewn about the scene, the ancient ruins are a romantic sight.

Xanthos was the capital of Ancient Lycia. The extensive site has a spectacular collection of ancient ruins *(below)*, including superb examples of Lycian tombs.

Europe England
LONDON

WHY GO *As summer draws to a close, London still promises endless thrills, from fabulous festivals to behind-the-scenes tours.*

Built on pomp and ceremony, London is now a cosmopolitan capital of dizzying diversity. Wherever you go, you'll find slices of life from every corner of the globe, from dazzling celebrations of Caribbean culture to unbeatable salt beef bagels on Brick Lane.

As the long summer comes to an end, London still fizzes with excitement. Days are warm, parks are mellow, and the lively hum of busy pubs pours out onto sidewalks. There are the last weeks of outdoor theater at Shakespeare's Globe; Proms in the Park brings the finale of the world's largest classical music festival to Hyde Park; and the Open House weekend offers a sneak peak inside some of the city's most exclusive addresses. What's more, many of the major museums and galleries are free, so there's no excuse not to soak up a bit of culture during your trip.

When Else to Go
December Christmas brings carol concerts, twinkling lights, and a giant Christmas tree to Trafalgar Square.

PLANNING YOUR TRIP **Getting there** Most international flights arrive into Heathrow and Gatwick airports. St. Pancras International connects to European high-speed railroads. **Getting around** London Underground and buses are frequent and reliable. **Weather** Mild and pleasant with occasional showers. **Average temperature** 57°F / 14°C.

UNMISSABLE MARKETS

Whether you're on the hunt for fashion, flowers, or street food, a visit to one of London's many markets is a must.

1 Spanning several streets and buildings, **Camden Market** deals in all things retro, including vintage fashion, vinyl, and quirky collectibles. There are also scores of food stalls dishing out authentic nosh from all over the world.

2 **Portobello Road** is home to London's liveliest street market. Browse antiques and bric-à-brac, plus food stalls, crafts, clothes, and music. Visit on Saturday to see the market in full swing.

3 London's oldest food market is also its most atmospheric. **Borough Market** has more than a hundred stalls selling high-quality produce from all over the country, as well as international specialities.

4 Londoners head east on Sunday mornings to peruse the teeming plant and flower market on **Columbia Road**. Each stall is a colorful cornucopia of all things horticultural.

5 Tiny **Maltby Street Market** is a favorite among locals. What it lacks in size, it more than makes up for in choice, with more than 30 artisan food and drink traders.

Clockwise from top left
Local eateries spill out
onto London streets;
contrasting architecture in
the City; the grand galleries
of Tate Britain; a guard
stands at attention on
Horse Guards Parade

Above Crossing a walkway through the rain forest canopy in Sabah, northern Borneo

Left The Labuk Bay monkey sanctuary; a Bornean orangutan, Tanjung Puting National Park

BORNEO

Asia Indonesia
BORNEO

WHY GO *Borneo's rain forests burst with fruit at this time of year, tempting orangutans down from the tree canopy. Join a jungle tour to glimpse the king of the swingers and other incredible wildlife.*

With its rocky pinnacles and misty rain forests, raging rivers, mangrove-encrusted shores, and coral reefs, Borneo is a living Eden. The third largest island in the world, it boasts a rich biodiversity and is home to around 15,000 species of flowering plants, including many rare orchids. Made up of Brunei, Malay, and Indonesian enclaves, Borneo is the center of evolution for many endemic forest species, including the Asian elephant, the Sumatran rhinoceros, and the clouded leopard. The rain forest, home to trees that tower to 246 ft (75 m), is also the natural habitat of the endangered Bornean orangutan, while the surrounding coastal waters support a magnificent ecosystem that abounds with marine life, corals, and species of turtles. Deforestation and the cultivation of palm oil continue to cause controversy, but pristine forests remain and are protected by conservation projects that rely on tourism.

Aside from jungle exploration, Borneo's incredible landscape also makes for great adventure sports, such as mountain climbing, rain forest trekking, and river rafting. Consider climbing Mount Kinabalu—you'll need to allow two days to climb and descend the mountain. If the sky is clear, the views from the summit are amazing. Whatever your Borneo adventure entails, the island's scenery and wildlife is undeniably spectacular.

When Else to Go
April After the monsoon season, this is a great time for relaxing on the beaches and jungle trekking.

PLANNING YOUR TRIP Getting there Kota Kinabalu is the island's main entry point, and Kota Kinabalu International Airport has regular flights from Kuala Lumpur and Singapore. Kuching International Airport is also well served. **Getting around** Buses connect the major sights. In towns, minibuses and taxis are usually plentiful. **Weather** Borneo enjoys a hot, tropical climate with some showers at this time of year. **Average temperature** 86°F / 30°C.

BEIJING

Asia China
BEIJING

WHY GO *Old meets new in China's charismatic capital city. September's cooler temperatures are a welcome relief after the muggy heat of the summer months.*

This vast, uncontainable city teems with people spilling out onto the streets to embrace the mellow temperature of the new season. The sheer size of Beijing's population is reflected in the monumental scale of the city's ancient imperial palaces and temple complexes. Take the Forbidden City: between its four towering walls, colossal courtyards linked by elaborate gateways are filled with lavish buildings, their roofs topped by a gilt menagerie of dragons, phoenixes, and other mythological beasts.

Not far from the busy streets and honking cars, there is tranquility among the city's ancient *hutongs*, meandering alleyways that are as old as the Forbidden City and often accessible only by rickshaw or bike. These untidy lanes and their timeless, crumbling courtyards form a communal living space for the locals where they can sit out and observe the world going by, gossip with their neighbors, play with their pets—including the occasional Pekinese dog—and enjoy games of chess, mahjong, and cards. But what is a *hutong* today could well be a skyscraper tomorrow, thanks to Beijing's insatiable appetite for change. The city's burgeoning arts and dining scene is transforming this ancient city into a cosmopolitan metropolis. Will you begin with ancient history or contemporary culture?

When Else to Go
February Chinese New Year celebrations take place across the city. **April** Spring brings milder weather, perfect for meandering the parks to see blossoming flowers.

PLANNING YOUR TRIP **Getting there** Beijing is served by Beijing Capital Airport. A rail link connects the airport to the city, and taxis are readily available. **Getting around** Beijing has cheap and efficient transportation options, including a subway, buses (with announcements in English), taxis, and, in tourist areas, rickshaws. **Weather** September sees relief from the heat of summer and the odd shower. **Average temperature** 68°F / 20°C.

The rooftops of Beijing's sprawling Forbidden City, with the modern city in the distance

Oceania New Zealand
QUEENSTOWN

QUEENSTOWN

WHY GO *It's spring on the South Island, and Queenstown's green valleys and snowcapped peaks offer all manner of outdoor activity.*

Welcome to Queenstown, the adventure capital of the world. This shoreside town is a vast, natural theme park where thrill seekers can enjoy bungee jumping, whitewater rafting, jet-boating, and countless other head-rush experiences. The town is also a premier ski destination, a snow sports playground set amid spectacular scenery, with the last of the snow available at this time of year.

It's not all thrills and spills, however. Queenstown welcomes spring in September, providing ample opportunity for more relaxed time spent outdoors. The landscape around the town bursts with cherry blossoms and daffodils, best enjoyed via a walk or a gentle bike ride. There are also a number of vineyards that open their doors and cellars in spring. Come the evening, join the Kiwis and dine alfresco, toasting the day's events with a crisp glass of the local Pinot Noir.

When Else to Go
June The ski season kicks off with the Winter Festival, a showcase of fireworks, music performances, comedy acts, sports competitions, and so much more.

PLANNING YOUR TRIP **Getting there** International flights arrive into Christchurch Airport, where you can catch a domestic flight to Queenstown or rent a car. **Getting around** Walking is the best way to get around the town, but a 4WD vehicle is recommended for beyond Queenstown. **Weather** Mild, but layers are advised. **Average temperature** 55°F / 13°C.

A snowboarder jumping on the slopes of Coronet Peak, Queenstown

MADEIRA

Europe Portugal
MADEIRA

WHY GO *In September, the weather is at its best, the crowds have thinned, and the countryside is blooming.*

Rising from the Atlantic like the mythical Atlantis, Madeira sits 620 miles (1,000 km) from Portugal's capital. In 1419, Portuguese adventurers exploring the coast of Africa recorded their fear as they headed for what they thought was the monster-infested rim of the ocean. What they found instead was paradise.

Lavishly decorated churches and luxurious rural mansions are the legacy of Madeira's early wealth. The scenery is as impressive as this art and architecture; you'll find tiny terraces clinging to the near-vertical valley sides, plus a plethora of tempting coves, forested ravines, and exotic blooms. In September, as the colors of the landscape begin to change and visitors become fewer, Madeira has the air of a secret garden, just waiting to be discovered.

When Else to Go
February–March The Carnival of Madeira sees colorful costumes and parades just before Easter.

PLANNING YOUR TRIP Getting there Madeira International Airport is about 30 minutes from the capital, Funchal. Madeira is also a popular port of call for cruise ships. **Getting around** Buses reach most parts of the island, but car rental gives flexibility. Taxis can be hired for day excursions. **Weather** Pleasantly warm with some showers. **Average temperature** 72°F / 22°C.

Pretty wildflowers on a hillside overlooking the North Atlantic Ocean, south-west Madeira

// OCTOBER

The sun rising over the
sweeping purple-hued fields
of Tuscany's Val d'Orcia

BUENOS AIRES

South America Argentina
BUENOS AIRES

WHY GO *Warm, spring days coupled with fewer tourists makes October an ideal time for soaking up the diversity and cultural depth of Buenos Aires.*

Entwined with the city's sights, parks, restaurants, and nightlife is something more intangible. You'll find it brushed in sensual strokes by tango dancers across the cobbled streets of the *barrios* (neighborhoods) of San Telmo and La Boca. Passionate fans shout it out from the bleachers in soccer stadiums. It drifts in the smoke of roasting meat at a *parrilla* (steak house) and shimmers in a glass of Argentina's renowned wine. Eva Perón embodied it back in the late 1940s and early 1950s. And the *porteños* (inhabitants of Buenos Aires) who patronize the trendy restaurants along the riverfront *barrio* of Puerto Madero and fill the bohemian bars in Palermo Viejo give it a contemporary twist.

Buenos Aires combines European style and sophistication with the South American gift of knowing how to have a good time. Come and see for yourself how this city mirrors the irrepressible spirit of Argentina.

When Else to Go
August Put on your dancing shoes at the World Tango Festival, a two-week event celebrating Argentina's famous dance.

PLANNING YOUR TRIP **Getting there** Flights arrive into Ezeiza International Airport, 22 miles (35 km) from the city center. **Getting around** The *subte* (metro) and buses are efficient; use taxis at night. **Weather** Warm, with plenty of sun. **Average temperature** 68°F / 20°C.

Left Dusk falling on colorful buildings and trees lining a pretty square in the historic *barrio* of La Boca

Below A sign for a tango bar in Buenos Aires, one of many in the city

Cypress trees and
cultivated hills in the
beautiful Val d'Orcia

TUSCANY

Europe Italy
TUSCANY

WHY GO *Harvesttime sees the rolling Tuscan hillsides draped in sunburned shades and romantic fall mists.*

Tuscany is a feast for the senses. Sublime art and breathtaking architecture vie for attention amid incomparably romantic landscapes. But in October, the region's rustic flavors take center stage. This is the season when porcini mushrooms and prized *tartufo* (truffles) flavor risottos, and game appears on local menus—slow-stewed wild boar or hare cooked with red wine and herbs, served with the region's wide pappardelle pasta.

Each area has its own specialty. Think of *bistecca alla fiorentina*—thick steak from the Valdiciana, drizzled with the finest olive oil and grilled over a chestnut-wood fire; Prato's *cantucci*, biscuits dipped in sweet Vin Santo; and *pici* pasta from the hill towns around Siena. Discover these authentic flavors as you tour the serene Tuscan countryside, or join a local cooking class and learn the secrets behind this region's sublime cuisine.

When Else to Go
May Enjoy balmy days, quiet beaches, and the many *sagre* (local food festivals) in the countryside.

PLANNING YOUR TRIP **Getting there** Tuscany's main airports are in Florence and Pisa. **Getting around** In cities, walk or use public transportation. Rent a car to tour the countryside. **Weather** Warm, but be prepared for rain and mist. **Average temperature** 68°F / 20°C.

A TASTE OF TUSCANY

1 **Cooking experiences** Boost your culinary credentials at one of the region's many cooking classes. Stop by San Lorenzo food market in Florence for a tour and pasta-making master class.

2 **Florentine street food** Traditionally made with tripe, *lampredotto* is Florence's most popular street food. Head to Nencioni on Piazza Mercato Nuovo to sample the best in town.

3 **White truffle market of Crete Senesi** Sleepy San Giovanni D'Asso springs to life during the white truffle season (November). Eat your fill of truffles at this market fair.

4 **Sagra della Bistecca** Every Tuscan town has its own food festivals (*sagre*), but not one beats Cortona's steak festival. Held every year in mid-August, it is the region's most important gastronomic event.

5 **Fine dining** Tuscany is home to some 35 Michelin-starred restaurants, where utterly delicious dishes are feasts for the eyes (*below*).

Bridges straddling
Florence's Arno River as
the sun sets over the city

Europe Hungary
BUDAPEST

WHY GO *As golden leaves color tree-lined terraces and the summer crowds begin to fade, join the locals in some good, clean fun.*

Straddling both sides of the Danube River, Hungary's capital is not one city but two: to the west, the medieval streets and imperial palaces of Buda; to the east, Pest, the commercial and political hub. Here, astoundingly ornate architecture abounds, a hark back to the Austro-Hungarian heyday, while grimy ruin bars are a staple of the city's nightlife.

Perhaps the biggest draw are the numerous thermal bathhouses. For a fizzing soak in an upmarket riot of Art Nouveau expression, head to the Gellért Baths. Or you may prefer the more humble Széchenyi Baths. Here, on the Pest side of town, you'll make waves with ordinary folk as they enjoy their daily treat—a hot bath, a game of chess, and a bottle of beer. Indulge in an invigorating massage, to help you really get under the skin of this city.

BUDAPEST

When Else to Go

April This is a great time to experience Hungarian folk traditions, including painting eggs at Easter. The weather is pleasant, and the city isn't yet overcrowded.

PLANNING YOUR TRIP **Getting there** International flights arrive into Ferenc Liszt Airport. **Getting around** Metro, buses, trams, and taxis operate throughout the city. **Weather** Mostly dry and sunny. **Average temperature** 61°F / 16°C.

Aerial view of Széchenyi Baths, the biggest bath complex in Europe

The grand Château de Chenonceau, shrouded in an eerie fog, seemingly floating on the water's still surface

LOIRE VALLEY

Europe France
LOIRE VALLEY

WHY GO *Explore French splendor in relative tranquility as summer tour groups diminish.*

European architecture doesn't get richer than the grand *châteaux* of the Loire Valley, circled by their historic moats. Reflecting the decadent beauty of the Renaissance, more than 50 15th- and 16th-century wildly extravagant mansions pepper the region.

Yet the Loire Valley is not just about stunning art and architecture. Dubbed "the Garden of France," the Loire is celebrated for its glorious gastronomy. Look for local apples and pears and, of course, the products of the Loire grapes, including great white wines such as Muscadet, Pouilly-Fumé, and Sancerre. Venture into troglodyte caves around Vouvray, Saumur, and Angers—home to the famous Saumur button mushrooms that fill the markets, where you can assemble a delectable picnic to enjoy as you tour this abundant region.

When Else to Go
May Early summer sees a little less rainfall and warmer days—perfect for a cycling trip.

PLANNING YOUR TRIP Getting there The area is served by two airports—Nantes-Atlantique and Tours Val de Loire. **Getting around** Public transportation is limited. Join a boat tour, cycle, or rent a car. **Weather** Mild, but be prepared for light rain. **Average temperature** 60°F / 16°C.

QUEENSLAND ISLAND ESCAPES

Scattered all along Queensland's coast are picture-perfect islands, with pristine beaches and stunning coral reefs. Here are four of our favorites.

Fraser Island Known as *K'gari* (meaning paradise) by local Aboriginal people, the world's largest sand island doesn't disappoint, with its gorgeous white beaches, lush rain forests, and clear lakes. You're also likely to encounter dingos, the island's most famous residents.

Lizard Island This remote island can be reached only by private charter. Located on the Great Barrier Reef between the inner and outer reef systems, the diving and snorkeling opportunities here are unparalleled. The underwater world is a kaleidoscope of color.

Heron Island Wildlife is everywhere here. The island's pisonia trees are home to thousands of birds, including noddy terns and muttonbirds. Between October and March, you can watch green and loggerhead turtles make their way up the beach to nest.

Whitsunday Island The highlight of this island *(below)* is the breathtaking Whitehaven Beach. Recognized as one of the world's best beaches, it has 6 miles (9 km) of pure white sand.

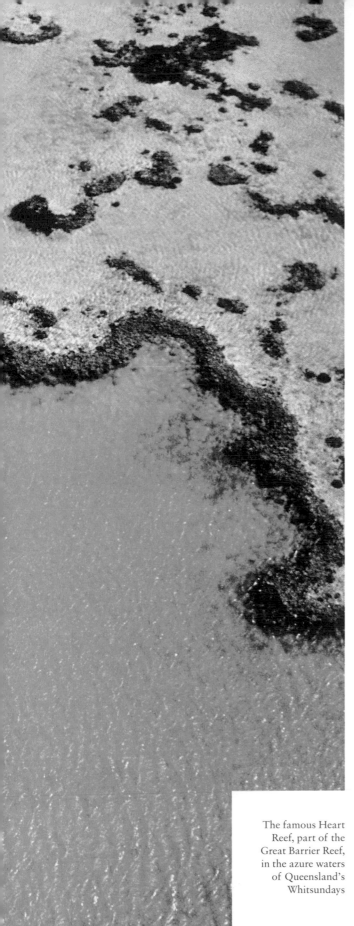

The famous Heart Reef, part of the Great Barrier Reef, in the azure waters of Queensland's Whitsundays

QUEENSLAND

Oceania Australia
QUEENSLAND

WHY GO *October is a great time to visit Australia's adventure playground. It's fairly quiet, and the weather is perfect—warm, pleasant, and ideal for long days spent outdoors.*

Queensland checks all the boxes for a sunny vacation destination, with soft, white-sand beaches and island hideaways, though thrill seekers may think that lounging around is a waste given the endless world-class adventure possibilities.

The coast overflows with opportunities for getting in and about the water, whether you are looking to go island-hopping on a gleaming yacht or to delve deep below sea level on a scuba dive. Divers bubble back to the surface from the Great Barrier Reef enthusing about the spectacular delights encountered below.

Inland, lush rain forests await. Venture into the dense foliage, and another Queensland unfolds, as exotic animal calls shriek out among ancient trees. Even here, activities are in abundance— tumble down raging rivers on a raft, ride the rapids on a kayak, or even fling yourself off a ridiculous height with only a rubber bungee for company.

When Else to Go
September Queensland's capital has an unbeatable buzz during the Brisbane Festival, with theater, music, dance, and circus shows.

PLANNING YOUR TRIP **Getting there** Flights arrive into Cairns and Brisbane. **Getting around** Rent a car or use the public buses. **Weather** Warm days and cool nights. **Average temperature** 77°F / 25°C.

ALBUQUERQUE

ALBUQUERQUE

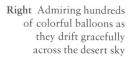

Right Admiring hundreds of colorful balloons as they drift gracefully across the desert sky

Below A balloon illuminated by its glowing burner; fiesta crowds enjoying the atmosphere

WHY GO *Held every October, the mass ascension of hundreds of multicolored hot-air balloons at Albuquerque International Balloon Fiesta never fails to leave onlookers breathless.*

It's a romantic picture—a single hot-air balloon sailing gracefully and silently across the sky. There's something uniquely enchanting about ballooning; the huge colorful orb just hangs in the air as if by magic. If one balloon is magical, seeing hundreds of them dotting the sky in an endless canvas of abstract shapes and vivid colors is beyond words. This is what happens every year at the thrilling Albuquerque International Balloon Fiesta, the largest convention of hot-air balloons in the world.

Those hoping to catch the best of the action rise at the crack of dawn, when more than 500 balloons in shapes previously unimagined lift off simultaneously, filling the barren desert sky as the crowds gaze in amazement from below. When you're

not staring up at the spectacle, weave your way through countless docked balloons, chat with pilots, capture breathtaking photographs, and sample traditional New Mexican fare, such as warm, puffy Navajo frybread and steaming tortilla soup, enjoying live music and entertainment as you eat. As night descends on the Rio Grande Valley, stand in awe of the Balloon Glow, as hundreds of balloons on the ground are illuminated all at once from the glow of their burners. Once the field clears, a spectacular fireworks display wraps up the evening with a bang.

When Else to Go
February Skiers visit Albuquerque to enjoy the slopes of the nearby Sandia Mountains.

PLANNING YOUR TRIP **Getting there** Balloon Fiesta Park is around 12 miles (19 km) north of Albuquerque Sunport, the state's only major airport. **Getting around** Most visitors rely on rental cars or the ABQ RIDE bus system. The New Mexico Rail Runner shuttles people to and from the park. **Weather** Generally dry. Cool in the morning and warm in the afternoon. **Average temperature** 70°F / 21°C.

MONTEREY

SANTA BARBARA

North America US
CALIFORNIA COAST

WHY GO *California's Highway 1 is hard to beat for driving pleasure, with the stretch from Monterey to Santa Barbara the most thrilling. The road is much quieter at this time of year.*

Highway 1 snakes along wave-lashed seashores, hugging the Golden State's coast all the way from the beautiful vineyards of Mendocino to just south of the sprawling metropolis of LA. Pick up a rental car in San Francisco and drive south 120 miles (200 km) to Monterey for the start of the most famous stretch of the drive. It's a classic route that winds on for 250 miles (400 km) to surf-city Santa Barbara. Along the way, you'll pass picturesque seaside towns, forests of towering redwoods, and Spanish missions that predate the state's founding. One minute, you're skimming alongside a golden beach caressed by smoothly curving sets of waves, and the next you're looking down onto thundering surf. But the drama really begins as you wind along the spectacularly scenic Big Sur, where waves smash ashore at the base of soaring mountains.

The landscape softens farther south; the mountains move inland, and cypress redwoods give way to palm trees and bougainvillea. Santa Barbara slips into view with its Spanish-style homes and surfer-dude chic. You'll have earned some rest and relaxation after a few days of driving, so enjoy some beach time here in Santa Barbara, indulge in a winery tour, and raise a glass of crisp, local Chardonnay.

When Else to Go
April–May Great weather and quieter beaches before the summer starts.

PLANNING YOUR TRIP **Getting there** San Francisco and LAX are both busy international airports and are well connected to their respective cities by train, bus, and taxi. **Getting around** Renting a car is the best option, although buses and Amtrak's Coast Starlight trains operate between LA and San Francisco. **Weather** Usually sunny and warm, although it can get quite hot inland. **Average temperature** 77°F / 25°C.

Crashing waves and foaming surf along a rugged outcrop of the beautiful Big Sur, California

Traditional dancing at dusk in the city of Oaxaca, in honor of the famous Day of the Dead celebrations

CITY HIGHLIGHTS

Cool and cultural, Oaxaca rivals the best of Latin America's cities. Here's how.

1

Gorgeous architecture in the form of Baroque churches and colorful, colonial-era buildings circle cobbled plazas.

2

Street art and bohemian bars abound. Embark on a hunt for murals by the likes of revered Lapiztola before evening tequilas.

3

Numerous markets sell freshly ground coffee, local mezcal, gorgeous woven baskets, and embroidered clothing. Perfect souvenirs.

OAXACA

Central America Mexico
OAXACA

WHY GO *Oaxaca is the best place to see Mexico's Day of the Dead celebrations, from October 31 to November 2.*

This most Mexican of fiestas is a truly supernatural event where the dead are believed to return to earth to commune with their living relatives. In the colonial city of Oaxaca and its surrounding indigenous villages, these ancient beliefs thrive, and the celebrations are at their most vivid. The reunion between the living and the dead is both joyful and poignant, and the atmosphere can be amazingly animated. To welcome their late relatives, families decorate loved ones' graves with flowers, candles, and miniature skulls. They spend hours in graveyards communing with the deceased, even staying for nightlong vigils. The sight of a cemetery glittering with candles and buzzing with chatter, and the dancing that accompany these reunions, will stay with you.

When Else to Go

July The Guelaguetza festival celebrates Oaxaca's indigenous communities with parades and performances.

PLANNING YOUR TRIP **Getting there** Oaxaca is 250 miles (400 km) southeast of Mexico City, with most travelers arriving via a domestic flight from Mexico City. **Getting around** There are plenty of taxis and buses. **Weather** Warm with the odd shower. **Average temperature** 77°F / 25°C.

North America US
KAUA'I

WHY GO *The Hawaiian island of Kaua'i is all about the sea and the lush, green nature inland. With the summer crowds gone, October is the perfect time to kick back and indulge in this tropical paradise.*

Kaua'i, nicknamed the "Garden Island," is covered with dense forests and myriad colorful flowers; it echoes with the twittering welcome of exotic birds while the hypnotic boom of waves crashing onto the golden beaches draws you in. Once a volcano rising from the sea, the island evolved into a breathtaking combination of rain forest, deserts, plains, and mountains. It is home to the Waimea Canyon, the largest canyon in the Pacific, and the Nā Pali Coast, featuring jungle-clad cliffs rising sharply from dark blue sea. Kaua'i is an intriguing place, created by the immense forces of nature and is still subject to them. Hollywood agrees and has used the unruly, primeval landscape as a back-drop in several films, including *King Kong* and *Jurassic World*.

The mountains, canyons, and beaches, especially on the Nā Pali Coast, are truly unique. To get a spectacular sea view, join a kayak tour and paddle around until the Nā Pali cliffs rear high above you. As you glide through the water, you'll be confronted with the same breathtaking spectacle the first Polynesians saw when they stumbled upon this natural paradise.

When Else to Go
September The Kaua'i Marathon and the Kaua'i Mokihana Festival, a weeklong celebration of Hawaiian culture, take place.

PLANNING YOUR TRIP **Getting there** Flights from the US mainland arrive in Lihu'e, the main city on Kaua'i. **Getting around** Renting a car is the best option. **Weather** October is warm; rainfall is frequent but short-lived. **Average temperature** 75°F / 24°C.

Sunshine dappling the jungle-clad cliffs of the Nā Pali Coast, with gentle waves lapping the golden shore

// NOVEMBER

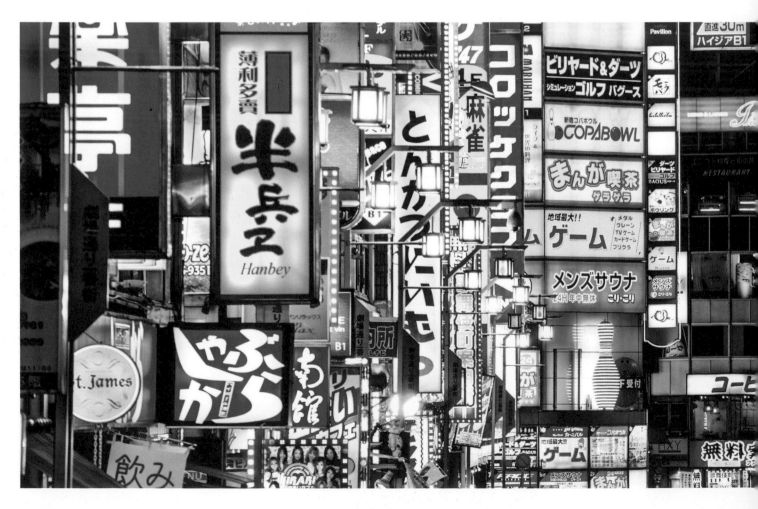

A riot of shining
neon lights in Shinjuku,
central Tokyo

VIETNAM

Asia
VIETNAM

WHY GO *With both captivating cities and time-forgotten countryside, Vietnam always rewards exploration. The start of the dry season brings uninterrupted pleasant days.*

With a blend of mesmerizing sights, sounds, smells, and tastes that is like no other, Vietnam delivers adventure and sensory overload. This is a land of picture-postcard images: a scattering of bobbing conical straw hats dotting a patchwork landscape of emerald rice fields; graceful girls in their elegant *ao dai* dresses, zipping around cities on motorcycles; and the dizzying colors of a Cao Dai temple. From a rich civilization with deeply held traditions has risen a country that has seen the future, and rushed headlong into it. The past, however, is always remembered, whether it be at ancient temples or the poignant sites of terrible 20th-century wars.

In contrast to other parts of Vietnam, the Mekong Delta seems untouched. The pace of life is slow in this lush, watery world of rice paddies, fish farms, and floating markets, where an intricate web of canals links tiny green islands on which all manner of tropical fruits grow.

Noisy, vibrant, chaotic, and colorful, Ho Chi Minh City dazzles, with its French colonial architecture and striking modern buildings. Tiny cafés line traffic-clogged streets; the smells of aromatic spices waft from countless restaurants and food stalls. Have a drink at the balcony bar of a high-rise hotel, and watch the city explode in a riot of neon—then get down there and join in.

When Else to Go
January–February Take part in Vietnam's extravagant Tet (Lunar New Year) celebrations.

Above Farmers walking through the terraced rice fields of Mu Cang Chai in northeast Vietnam

Right A boat paddling through the Mekong Delta; dining out in Ho Chi Minh City

---

PLANNING YOUR TRIP **Getting there** Hanoi is served by Nôi Bài International Airport, and Ho Chi Minh City has Tân Son Nhát International Airport. **Getting around** Cyclos, *xe om* (motorcycles), and taxis zip around the towns; buses, trains, and planes cover longer distances. **Weather** Dry, but humidity is high. **Average temperature** 81°F / 27°C.

PICTURE PERFECT

1 **Tokyu Plaza Omotesando Harajuku** Snap a kaleidoscope-like image of this multistory shopping complex from the top of the mirror-encased escalator as you exit.

2 **Nakagin Capsule Tower** Take a picture of this modular building from across the street. Resembling a stack of washing machines, it's a rare example of Japanese Metabolism.

3 **Shibuya Crossing** Grab a coffee at Shibuya Tsutaya's glass-fronted Starbucks, then make a beeline for the second floor, the best place to get a shot of the famous Shibuya Crossing.

4 **Golden Gai** Home to a maze of 200 tiny bars, the six narrow alleyways of Golden Gai are like a portal to a distant time. Venture here after dark to snap photos of buzzy bar life.

5 **Sensō-ji Temple** Open 24 hours a day, you can capture this peaceful Buddhist temple complex (*below*) at all hours. Come just before dawn for the perfect shot of the sun rising over the Kaminarimon (Thunder Gate).

Bright and colorful neon signs overlooking a busy zebra crossing in the ward of Shinjuku, in Tokyo

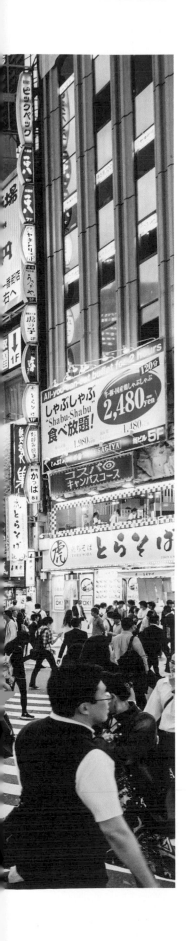

TOKYO

Asia Japan
TOKYO

WHY GO *With pleasant days, clear skies, and a stunning backdrop of golden foliage, November is a great time to visit this modern metropolis where the past and future collide.*

Nowhere in the world combines the ancient and modern quite like Tokyo. On the one hand, it's a futuristic neon cityscape, fast-paced and crowded, with a high-octane lifestyle. Think swarms of worker bees crossing the Shibuya intersection, all of them talking into high-tech cell phones while animated advertising hoardings bombard them with strobe-effect slogans. On the other hand, there are quiet cobbled side streets leading to secluded Shinto shrines and Buddhist temples, where Tokyoites can grab a rare moment of quiet contemplation, before continuing with their busy daily lives.

While shopping, dining, and the bright lights of the entertainment district remain the superficial attractions of big-city Tokyo life, the most rewarding experiences are far simpler: admiring the chrysanthemums on a walk in the Imperial Palace East Garden, eating a hearty bowl of noodles at a street-side stall, and watching children play with fall leaves at a backstreet shrine. Such sights are a humble reminder that while Tokyo appears to be the ultimate 21st-century city, bustling and jostling into the future, scratch beneath its brash veneer and you'll soon see that the traditional

values of Japanese society—nature, family, and philosophy—are still very much alive.

When Else to Go
March–April Instead of fall leaves, you'll find delicate cherry blossoms in Tokyo's parks.

PLANNING YOUR TRIP **Getting there** Narita International Airport is 40 miles (66 km) from downtown. **Getting around** The extensive underground system is cheap and efficient. **Weather** Cool and dry. **Average temperature** 59°F / 15°C.

Yakitori restaurants on Memory Lane in Tokyo

BURGUNDY

Europe France
BURGUNDY

WHY GO *Take a cruise on this golden region's canals at harvesttime to sample its bountiful delights, from fiery mustard to warming wine.*

Brimming with good food and fine wine, Burgundy is France's heartiest region. In November, the hunting season is underway, mushrooms are being gathered, and the grape harvest is being celebrated, making it the perfect time to chug along the 150-mile (242 km) Canal de Bourgogne in a canal boat, stopping off at tasting rooms, picturesque villages, and idyllic picnic spots.

Alternatively, cycle or stroll through the burnished gold forests and ruddy vineyards. Once you've worked up an appetite, sample Dijon's famous mustard, comforting *boeuf bourguignon*, or wild mushrooms, newly gathered, all washed down with a glass of Chablis, Côte de Nuits, or Côte de Beaune.

When Else to Go
July The Festival International d'Opéra Baroque sees Baune host operas, concerts, and recitals every weekend.

PLANNING YOUR TRIP **Getting there** Dijon's airport is 4 miles (6 km) south of the city. Canal tours depart from Paris and Dijon. **Getting around** Apart from by canal, the main towns are linked by bus. **Weather** Cold in the evenings. **Average temperature** 43°F / 6°C.

The *Queen of the Mississippi* in early morning mist

Fall mist blanketing a vineyard in Burgundy

North America US
MISSISSIPPI CRUISE

WHY GO *Mild weather makes fall the perfect time to enjoy both the river and onshore activities to the full without the summer's humidity.*

NEW ORLEANS

The mighty Mississippi is the largest river in the US. Countless literary and musical masterpieces have been inspired by it over the years, but the true folklife of America has its roots firmly grounded in the lower Mississippi. From New Orleans, as you cruise along the river, the history of the South unfolds.

The elegantly appointed, six-deck *Queen of the Mississippi* paddle-wheel steamboat makes the journey from the port of New Orleans to Oak Alley Plantation—the grand residence used in the opening scene of the Deep South classic *Gone with the Wind*. Then she sails on to the quaint town of Natchez, where you can hop straight off the boat into 19th-century

America. Packed with history, this is the oldest European settlement on the Mississippi River. The next stop is historic Vicksburg, Mississippi, where the National Military Park captures the spirit of the Civil War. Explore the Vicksburg battlefield where more than 1,300 monuments, fortifications, and a restored Union gunboat tell the story of those who lost their lives here.

Farther down river lies Baton Rouge, Louisiana's sleepy state capital, where historic buildings reflect the city's French Creole roots. Soon it's time to return to the 21st century as the boat chugs back to New Orleans and the bustling streets of the French Quarter.

When Else to Go
February–March During Mardi Gras, New Orleans becomes one big party.

PLANNING YOUR TRIP **Getting there** New Orleans is a good place to start a cruise and is served by Louis Armstrong International Airport. **Getting around** Tours from the cruise are included as part of the *Queen of the Mississippi* package. **Weather** Mainly clear. **Average temperature** 61°F / 16°C.

Bukchon Hanok
Village, with
Seoul's modern
buildings and
mountains beyond

SEOUL

Asia South Korea
SEOUL

WHY GO *Seoul has soul in November. While the city pulses, the surrounding mountains provide a peaceful retreat, with walking trails and trees ablaze with the colors of fall.*

Seoul is a city of contrasts, where glimmering skyscrapers loom above timeless Buddhist temples and leafy parks. The capital distills the essence of everything that is enchanting about South Korea. Days spent exploring the traditional streets of Bukchon Hanok and art galleries of Leeum Samsung turn into nights necking *soju* in a rooftop bar, with K-pop providing a thumping soundtrack.

All the while, standing silent guard as the city rushes on, are Seoul's mighty mountains, their forested slopes a playground for walkers. November is the perfect time to get out in nature—the humid summer has given way to pleasantly cool fall weather, and the forested hills erupt in a riot of fiery reds, yellows, and ambers. Bukhansan is crisscrossed with gentle forest trails that reward your efforts with incredible views of the metropolis. Sound too

much like hard work? Namsan, in the heart of the city, combines stellar views over the city with the added convenience of a cable car. If you prefer to stay closer to sea level, stroll the riverside boardwalks of Hangang Park, or get lost amid the trees, lakes, and flowers of Seoul Forest.

You'll have worked up an appetite after all that fresh air, and Seoul's celebrated food scene won't disappoint, especially as November welcomes the Seoul Kimchi Festival, with street stalls serving up bowls of the spicy delicacy. Day or night, mountains or megalopolis, South Korea's capital is utterly spellbinding.

When Else to Go
April Pink cherry blossom blankets temples and parks. **December** The snow-covered temples and palaces are particularly atmospheric.

PLANNING YOUR TRIP **Getting there** Seoul is served by Incheon International Airport, around 30 miles (48 km) from the city, and is connected by AREX train, bus, and taxi. **Getting around** A subway system connects most neighborhoods, and there are trains and buses. **Weather** Fairly cool with some rainfall. **Average temperature** 45°F / 7°C.

PARKS AND WALKING TRAILS

1 **Seoul Forest** was opened in 2005 as a symbol of Seoul's commitment to green space. It is a great spot for a stroll or bike ride.

2 **Banpo Hangang Park** is loved for the technicolor Banpo Bridge Rainbow Fountain and is popular for chimaek—fried chicken and beer.

3 The **Changdeokgung grounds** were the pleasure gardens of kings in a bygone era, and today the palace grounds remain a peaceful sanctuary.

4 **Namsan Park** represents Seoul's contrasts: rich in trees, trails, and wildlife but crested by the modern N Seoul Tower.

5 **Bukhansan National Park** (*below*) has winding mountain trails, which make for lovely hiking, especially along the fortress walls.

AITUTAKI

Oceania Cook Islands
AITUTAKI

WHY GO *The end of "winter" in the Cook Islands is the perfect time to visit this technicolor paradise, without the threat of rain dampening your spirits.*

It's said that the Cook Islands, and particularly Aitutaki, are what Tahiti was 50 years ago: a place of such beauty and purity that it cannot fail to fill visitors with complete awe.

Aitutaki sits at the apex of a vast lagoon dotted by tiny islands called *motus*. "Blue" is the color usually applied to South Sea water, but Aitutaki only begins at "blue"—the lagoon forms a quilt of unmodulated patches in every shade imaginable of blue and green: emerald, aquamarine, cobalt, Prussian blue, royal blue, and periwinkle. Below the water, the color palette turns psychedelic with vivid corals that are eclipsed only by resident fish that seem to have dipped themselves in a paintbox: reds, oranges, royal blues, canary yellows, turquoise—sometimes all on the same fish. On land, this riot continues: the bold, seductive reds of the immortelle trees; the woven floral crowns that people wear in their hair; and the sensual shades and perfumes in the

The crystal clear waters and white sands of the lagoon framing Aitutaki

leis (flower garlands) thrown around visitors' necks when they arrive in this painting brought to life.

When Else to Go
September See humpback whales close to shore as they pass by the Cook Islands on their journey to warmer waters.

PLANNING YOUR TRIP **Getting there** Air Rarotonga has daily flights to Aitutaki from the international airport on Rarotonga. **Getting around** You can easily explore on foot, but cars, scooters, and bikes can be rented. **Weather** Warm and dry. **Average temperature** 84°F / 29°C.

SNORKELING SPOTS

An abundance of marine life and colorful coral landscapes thrive in the underwater world that separates the Cook Islands from one another, making the scenery beneath the water's surface just as impressive as that on dry land.

1 **Aroa Lagoon Marine Reserve**, on the main island of Rarotonga, is home to impressive reefs.

2 Isolated **Muri Lagoon** is reachable only by kayak from Muri Beach, but it's worth the journey.

3 Sheltered **Aitutaki Lagoon** is known for its clear waters and sheer abundance of colorful sea life.

4 The volcanic landscape of **Black Rock**, Rarotonga, looks otherworldly from beneath the water.

5 **One Foot Island**, near Aitutaki, is an underwater metropolis due to its deep channels.

Oceania Australia
TASMANIA

WHY GO *With mild spring days, blooming wildflowers, and long daylight hours, this is the ideal time to pack your bags, don your hiking boots, and discover what "Tassie" has to offer.*

It's easy to feel humbled by the enormity of Tasmania's wild and remote location. Virtually at the edge of the world, there's just the vast expanse of the mighty Southern Ocean separating this spectacular tract of wilderness from the Antarctic continent. To the west, it's some 12,000 miles (20,000 km) to the next landmass—South America. Such isolation has been a lifeline for the island's native flora and fauna, and the island has millions of acres of wild countryside to explore.

Tasmania is covered in managed walking tracks, including the famed Overland Track—a 40-mile (65-km), six-day walk through its rugged alpine heart. On the Freycinet Peninsula, the short but thoroughly rewarding 45-minute uphill trek to the Wineglass Bay Lookout provides a heart-stopping view of one of the planet's most spectacular stretches of sand.

On the west of the island, in the glacial lakes and streams of the Franklin-Gordon Wild Rivers National Park, there are links with the Permian period, some 250 million years ago. Primitive crustaceans still live here among the rivers and ferns they've called home for millions of years. The Franklin River, one of three major rivers that run through the park, is revered by Tasmanians for its natural, cultural, and historical significance. Experience its beauty and isolation on a rafting excursion with a local guide.

Off the usual tourist trail, Tasmania is Australia's best-kept secret, offering endless possibilities for adventure in an ancient landscape that teems with life.

When Else to Go
January Summer is festival time, with foodies' favorite Taste of Tasmania and the pumping Falls Festival, MONA FOMA, and Cygnet Folk Festival.

PLANNING YOUR TRIP **Getting there** There are flights to Hobart from Melbourne, Adelaide, Sydney, Brisbane, and Canberra. Ferries make regular overnight trips from Melbourne to Devonport on the north coast. **Getting around** Touring is best done with a car. **Weather** Generally warm and dry. **Average temperature** 68°F / 20°C.

A path winding through the wonderfully wild scenery of Cradle Mountain National Park, Tasmania

BAHAMAS

Caribbean
BAHAMAS

WHY GO *Fringed by pristine sand and teal-blue lagoons, the Bahamas are a beachgoer's delight in November. For the more adventurous, there is so much more to be discovered.*

This chain of tranquil isles—some large, others tiny—is sprinkled across a vast area of blue-green western Atlantic waters. Each group is as distinct as a thumbprint. Island-hopping from one to the next, visitors discover that even the most Lilliputian island is blessed with gargantuan charm.

Nassau, the capital, with its plethora of hotels and restaurants, provides a perfect combination of fine beaches and aquatic adventures that appeal to the young and young at heart. Choose from a range of activities—from aquabiking to sunfish-boat sailing—at Cable Beach. You can even take to the air for a bird's-eye view of Nassau and neighboring Paradise Island.

Once you've had your fill of energetic escapades, it's time to hit the beach for some much-needed downtime. There are, of course, plenty to choose from, but few can rival Eleuthera's Harbour Island, or Briland as it's known to locals, famous for its pink sands merging into the electric-blue water. One of the Family Islands, Briland, with its pastel clapboard cottages, is the ultimate picture-postcard. Peek into its tiny churches, indulge in traditional seafood restaurants, and rent a golf cart to explore the island. And after all that, submerge yourself in the turquoise waters and soak up that hot Bahamian sun.

When Else to Go
January Junkanoo, the mother of all street parties, takes place across the islands on New Year's Day.

PLANNING YOUR TRIP **Getting there** Fly into Lynden Pindling International Airport, then board domestic flights, ferries, and mailboats to reach the other islands. **Getting around** There are many modes of transportation around the islands, including car, boat, and rented bicycles. Taxis are readily available. **Weather** Sunny with cooling trade winds. **Average temperature** 79°F / 26°C.

A wooden pier stretching out from Pink Sands Beach

RAJASTHAN

Asia India
RAJASTHAN

WHY GO *The summer heat has passed, making this the perfect time to discover the legacy of the magical state of Rajasthan. Journey through gorgeous scenery on board the Palace on Wheels train.*

A majestic land of fairy-tale palaces and vibrant local life, Rajasthan fulfills all expectations of India. There is no more appropriate way of traveling through India than by train, and the opulent Palace on Wheels provides a truly unforgettable trip from Delhi to Agra. Chugging leisurely through Rajasthan allows you to revel in the scenery, comprising lush fields, tropical forests, and stunning palaces.

This land is home to rajas and maharajas, and their culture and history will delight curious travelers who wish to experience India's past and present. In this desert kingdom, fortresses wrap themselves around hills, while in the plains below, pleasure gardens surround serene lakeside fortresses. Passing through the ornate gates of Rajasthan's palaces means stepping into a world that encompasses the folk traditions and vivid history of this

enchanting state. Here, you'll discover treasures that tell stories of those who have peopled these historic abodes through the generations. Luxury still pervades, even today; meander through marble hallways, indulge in fine cuisine, and admire the exquisite heirlooms found at every turn.

The pace of the Palace on Wheels trip provides ample time to explore the state's memorable palaces and unwind in your own lavish cabin, or socialize with a cocktail in the sumptuous dining carriage. On board this luxurious train, you're in for a trip of a lifetime.

When Else to Go
March Rajasthan celebrates Gangaur, a festival honoring Gauri or Parvati, the Hindu goddess of fertility, love, beauty, and marriage.

PLANNING YOUR TRIP **Getting there** Delhi's Indira Gandhi International Airport, in the state of Uttar Pradesh, is the main entry point, though Jaipur and Jodhpur both have airports. **Getting around** There are regular trains from Delhi to cities and towns throughout Rajasthan. The Palace on Wheels travels from Delhi through Rajasthan and onto Agra between October and March. Towns and cities have taxis, cycle rickshaws, and auto rickshaws. **Weather** Dry with a more bearable heat. **Average temperature** 91°F / 33°C.

Above A monkey running along the walls of Jaipur's Amber Fort

Right A woman standing under an intricate pavilion on Gadi Sagar Lake in Jaisalmer

// DECEMBER

Cockle pickers aboard
their boats on
Vembanad Lake, Kerala

TORTOLA

Caribbean British Virgin Islands
TORTOLA

WHY GO *Reliably sunny skies and balmy temperatures are hard to resist in December. Tortola possesses all the key ingredients for a relaxing winter getaway.*

Tortola is a place of repose, with beaches rivaling in beauty and solitude those of anywhere in the world. The island is scalloped by secluded coves, and the north shore is fringed with endless stretches of champagne-colored beaches: Brewers Bay, Cane Garden Bay, Elizabeth Beach, and Long Bay are some of the loveliest.

Carefree and casual, Tortola has many great restaurants and bars that are perfect for lingering lunches and alfresco candlelit dinners. Dine on velvety crab callaloo and johnnycakes (a spicy okra stew with cornbread) as you listen to the calming sounds of lapping waves. Later, head down to one of the many beach bars scattered around the bays and, with a potent rum cocktail in hand, dance the night away on the shore to the calypso music that throbs across the moonlit bay.

When you feel in need of some activity, take a trip to Road Town, Tortola's urban hub. The town is still steeped in its colonial past, with elegant wooden houses and an old-worldly feel. Stroll down the central shopping strip, narrow Main Street, and pick up some of the beautiful gold, emeralds, and shells that Tortola is famed for, before taking the weight off your feet with a long lunch. If you're feeling adventurous, rent one of the motor-boats bobbing alongside the jetties and explore the neighboring islands that seem to float invitingly on the horizon. A sunset stroll along the sands is the perfect way to conclude the day.

When Else to Go

March–April The BVI Spring Regatta welcomes sailboats for a week of sailing contests.

PLANNING YOUR TRIP **Getting there** International visitors can fly into San Juan (Puerto Rico) or Santo Domingo (Dominican Republic) and catch a connecting flight. **Getting around** There are plenty of taxis, or you can rent a car. Water taxis, ferries, and small charter planes link Tortola to the other British Virgin Islands. **Weather** Tortola enjoys balmy weather with gentle, cooling trade winds. **Average temperature** 84°F / 29°C.

Waves lapping along
a palm-lined shore
on Tortola

VIENNA

Europe Austria
VIENNA

WHY GO *A visit over Christmas will give you a chance to enjoy the fabulous festive markets and dance the night away at the party in St. Stephen's Square on New Year's Eve.*

Of all the cities in Europe, Vienna has the merriest Advent and Christmas imaginable, one that lasts for weeks and weeks, starting with the arrival of St. Nicholas and his scary sidekick Krampus at the Christkindlmarkt.

Every year for centuries, Vienna has transformed into a winter wonderland with lights twinkling in the frosty nights and open-air Christmas markets popping up all over the city. These colorful markets sell a huge selection of beautifully made handicrafts, toys, decorations, and tree ornaments, all carefully displayed. As you wander through the maze of stalls, the smell of roasted chestnuts, *Glühwein* (hot spiced wine), *Punsch* (fruit punch spiked with wine), and *Lebkuchen* (a molded gingerbread) drifts through the air, tempting you to try the Christmas fare for which the Viennese markets are famed.

When it comes to tradition, Vienna pulls out all the stops—there are choirs that fill the city with song, special marionette shows, and an immense display of Nativity scenes. After a traditional Christmas, the party goes on. New Year's Eve in Vienna is one big celebration—a huge market extends along a mile-long strip linking the city's squares. The heart of the party is in the plaza around St. Stephen's Cathedral, where revelers sip chilled champagne and dance into the night.

And there's more. New Year's Eve is merely a prelude to 300 balls that take place during January's Ball Season. There's nothing more quintessentially Viennese than a ball, so a waltz around the dance floor is the perfect end to your time in the city.

When Else to Go

September–October This is a great time to visit, as the summer crowds have gone, the air is crisp and clear, and there are plenty of cultural events, such as the Viennale Film Festival and the Long Night of Museums.

Above The Christkindlmarkt, with its loaded stalls and festive lights, on Rathausplatz in front of Vienna's town hall

Right Glasses of warm *Glühwein*; decorated gingerbread on sale at the Christkindlmarkt; beautiful Christmas decorations twinkling in soft lighting

PLANNING YOUR TRIP **Getting there** International flights arrive into Vienna International Airport, 12 miles (20 km) southeast of the city. **Getting around** The best way to see Vienna is on foot. There is also a subway system (U-Bahn), as well as buses and trams. **Weather** December is cold, with some light snow. **Average temperature** 37°F / 3°C.

A traditional houseboat gliding along the beautiful palm-shaded backwaters of Kerala

KERALA

Asia India
KERALA

WHY GO *It's during December that Kerala lives up to its nickname, "God's Own Country." The monsoon has ended, leaving a lush landscape in its wake. This is best seen by a trip through Kerala's backwaters.*

Still, green waters, channeled through rice paddies and dense coconut groves, only occasionally disturbed by the languid movement of a *kettuvallam* (rice barge)—these are the palm-shaded lakes that make up Kerala's 560-mile (900-km) network of backwaters, a patchwork of land and water. Life here has remained distinctly rural, with locals living alongside animals and vegetable plots, worlds away from India's sprawling cities.

There is no more appropriate way to travel through these lush waterways than by *kettuvallam*, passing centuries-old fishing communities and abundant plantations at a leisurely pace. Originally used to ferry rice, these attractive wooden boats now meander through the waterways, shuttling children to and from school and delivering produce to local villages.

As the sun sets over the backwaters, silhouetting the palms against the sky, a deep peace settles, broken only by the occasional shriek of a monkey. This is an utterly enchanting experience, unlike anything else on the subcontinent.

When Else to Go
January–February The weather remains warm and dry.
August–September Boat races are held for the festival of Onam.

PLANNING YOUR TRIP **Getting there** International flights arrive into Kochi and the state capital, Thiruvananthapuram. **Getting around** Use buses, trains, or hire a driver (agree on a fee first). You can see the backwaters only by boat. **Weather** It's balmy, with the monsoon finishing at the start of the month. **Average temperature** 86°F / 30°C.

A stingray swimming along the sandy sea floor, just beneath the water's surface, off the coast of Grand Cayman

CAYMAN
ISLANDS

Caribbean
CAYMAN ISLANDS

WHY GO *Warm waters, crystal clear visibility, and stunning marine life—December is the perfect time to visit these Caribbean islands for sensational scuba-diving excursions.*

The cobalt-blue waters framing the Cayman Islands conceal a breath-taking underwater world studded with flashing shoals of brightly colored fish, dazzling coral reef formations, and eerie shipwrecks. This is a scuba diver's paradise. The dramatic, submerged landscape around the islands hosts more than 150 superb dive spots, each with its own distinct character and catering to all levels of ability. There are night dives, day dives, wreck dives, cave dives—the choice is dizzying.

Avid divers shouldn't miss Cayman Brac, the farthest east of the three main islands and home to one of the Caribbean's most sensational dive spots. Here, the famed North Wall drops away to an astonishing 14,000 ft (4,250 m), while the steeper and more awesome South Wall drops away farther still, into the velvet blackness of the precipice below. The walls are alive with sponges, finger corals, sea fans, and an incredible diversity of marine life, which includes moray eels, parrotfish, stingrays, and green sea turtles. Less intrepid divers might prefer to opt for the excellent shallow dives nearby, which lead divers through caves and tunnels and out across canyons and sublime towers of coral reef, where, on particularly clear days, the visibility can reach up to 150 ft (46 m). Dive into the blue and see for yourself.

When Else to Go
March Prices drop and the weather is lovely. **June** Swimmers race one mile as part of the Flowers Sea Swim.

PLANNING YOUR TRIP **Getting there** The international airport on Grand Cayman is the main arrival point. Little Cayman has daily interisland flights. Cruise ships stop regularly. **Getting around** Rental cars, motorcycles, and bicycles are available on Grand Cayman and Cayman Brac; bicycles and 4WD vehicles on Little Cayman. Taxis are plentiful. **Weather** Warm, clear skies, and little rain. **Average temperature** 82°F / 28°C.

MARINE LIFE

The turquoise-blue waters that surround the Cayman Islands support a dazzling array of marine life. Keep your eyes peeled for these aquatic critters.

Particularly plentiful in the waters around Grand Cayman, the multicolored **parrotfish** *(above)*, with its beak-like mouth, helps to keep the coral clean and healthy while it feeds.

The Caribbean reef shark *(above)* is a fairly common sight in deeper channels of water near Little Cayman and Cayman Brac.

Diving and snorkeling are hugely popular on this island paradise. The ultimate reward? A rare sighting of an elusive **green sea turtle** *(above)* in the wild.

An astronomer studying
the Milky Way in the
Atacama Desert

South America Chile
SAN PEDRO DE ATACAMA

WHY GO *Reach for the stars in northern Chile. December is the last month of spring, promising warm temperatures, fewer crowds, and clear skies—the ideal conditions for stargazing in the desert.*

Shimmering salt flats and surreal rock formations, gushing geysers and emerald-green lakes, looming volcanoes and sheer-faced mountains, all watched over by stellar skies—welcome to San Pedro de Atacama, the driest desert on earth. Northern Chile's geography and lack of light pollution make this a truly heavenly place for stargazing. December is a glorious time to look up to San Pedro's night sky, glistening with stars, planets, constellations, nebulas, clusters, and other celestial bodies. It's also quieter at this time of year, so you'll feel like you have the entire cosmos to yourself.

Stargazing tours provide an illuminating insight into the night sky, with astronomer guides showing you how to read a "sky map" and pick out glittering stars, constellations, and galaxies. Squint through telescopes to catch a glimpse of Jupiter, Saturn and its rings, and the Andromeda Galaxy, and use the special equipment provided to take your own incredible photos of the colossal cosmos stretching overhead.

A stargazing tour is best combined with a visit to the cutting-edge Atacama Large Millimeter Array (ALMA), the world's largest radio telescope. This remarkably powerful piece of technology allows astronomers to study the origins of the universe and the formation of the first galaxies. To us mere mortals, it's a mind-expanding experience; outer space will never feel so close at hand.

When Else to Go
June The lively Fiesta de San Pedro y San Pablo (Feast of Saint Peter and Saint Paul) takes place on June 29, with music, dancing, parades, and lots of food and drink.

PLANNING YOUR TRIP **Getting there** The nearest airport—El Loa—is in the city of Calama, 62 miles (100 km) northwest of San Pedro. Regular buses run from El Loa to San Pedro. **Getting around** You can walk, cycle, take a taxi, or rent a car to visit some nearby sights, but organized tours are the best way to explore the region. **Weather** Warm with occasional light showers. **Average temperature** 75°F / 24°C.

"This is a world of glistening white, broken only by the intensely vivid colors of woolly winter hats."

Left Reindeer walking through the snowy landscape of Lemmenjoki National Park, Lapland

Above A cozy campfire in Lapland; snow-topped trees and a cute cabin

LAPLAND

HELSINKI

Europe Finland
HELSINKI AND LAPLAND

WHY GO *No one does Christmas like the Finns. Visitors to the capital, Helsinki, will find festive cheer at every turn. Continue on to Lapland for sugar-coated, childish jollity—this is, after all, the home of Santa Claus.*

The Finns love winter and the trappings of Christmas that come hand in hand with the season. They revel in it and invite the world to join them on frozen ponds and ski slopes. It's so cold that sometimes the sea even freezes over and brave locals don their ice skates. This is a world of glistening white, broken only by the intensely vivid colors of woolly winter hats, scarves, and mittens.

The best place to start a festive Finnish foray is in the capital, Helsinki, a city that has both the style of its Nordic neighbors and the romance of Eastern Europe. Here, you'll discover glittering fairy lights, magical markets, Christmas carols, and festive shows galore.

But you can't come all this way and not visit Santa in Finnish Lapland. By early December, holiday sights, sounds, and aromas fill the land: the excited squeal of children catching a glimpse of Santa, sausages and herring sizzling over glowing coals, the aroma of freshly baked honey cakes as you enter a café, mellow brass notes from a street musician's horn, and the hubbub of open-air markets filled with shoppers. At least one booth will have a steaming cauldron of *glögi*, a mouth-tingling brew of red wine, spices, raisins, and black currant juice that warms you to your toes. This really is a winter wonderland for little and big kids alike.

When Else to Go
February Lapland is buried in snow, and the magical Northern Lights often make an appearance. **September** The trees shed their foliage in Helsinki, known locally as *"ruska."*

PLANNING YOUR TRIP **Getting there** Flights arrive into Helsinki Airport, 12 miles (20 km) from the city center. **Getting around** Buses, trams, trains, and boats offer comprehensive transportation in Helsinki. Lapland is 515 miles (830 km) north and can be reached by an 11-hour train ride or a domestic flight. **Weather** Cold with frequent light snow. **Average temperature** 28°F / –2°C.

LAOS

Asia
LAOS

WHY GO *December's clear and bright skies provide the perfect backdrop for seeing the sights of Laos while traveling down the fast-flowing Mekong.*

Situated high in the mist-shrouded mountains of northern Laos, Luang Prabang, once the royal capital, sits on a promontory on the broad Mekong River. It remains a treasure trove of ornately carved wooden temples, covered with golden stencils and shimmering mosaics, with cascading multitiered roofs.

There is no better way to arrive in Luang Prabang than by boat on the Mekong, a memorable journey that starts at the Thai border. Sailing down its swirling waters, past sheer limestone cliffs and jungle-clad mountains, unspoiled land-scapes, picturesque villages, and sacred caves come into view.

Continue down the river to Vientiane, Laos's laid-back capital. The peace here is broken by tuk-tuks rattling along to the morning market where visitors bargain for dazzling raw silk and silver jewelry. In the evening, watch the spectacular sunset turn the Mekong from red to gold and reflect on this little-changed land.

When Else to Go
April Boun Pi Mai (Lao New Year) is celebrated across three days, with ceremonies, parades, boat races, and lots of water.

PLANNING YOUR TRIP **Getting there** Fly to Thailand's Chiang Mai International Airport and travel to Chiang Khong to cross the border into Laos. Take a bus to Huay Xai (marked Bokeo) and head to the pier to board your boat. **Getting around** The stops en route are best explored on foot. **Weather** Dry and hot. **Average temperature** 86°F / 30°C.

Clockwise from top left
Riverboat on the Mekong at sunset; money offerings outside a Buddhist temple in Vientiane; young Buddhist monks walking by Wat Siphoutabath, Luang Prabang

North America US
SANTA FE

(map of the United States with Santa Fe marked)

SANTA FE

WHY GO *Christmas celebrations occur throughout the month, but don't miss the dazzlingly unique Santa Fe festivities from December 23 to 26.*

It's a simple thing really, a candle, in a paper bag, filled with sand. Light the candle at dusk, and the little lantern, known as a *farolito*, glows with a warm, inviting light. Now imagine the tens of thousands that line the city's roads and windowsills of the buildings.

Christmas in Santa Fe is, of course, more than *farolitos*. It's the traditions that reach back hundreds of years and celebrate Santa Fe's powerful and captivating blend of Native American, Spanish, and Anglo cultures. It's the cold, clear nights, where the air seems so transparent that you can see forever and the starlit night sky dazzles from horizon to horizon like an inverted bowl of celestial fairy lights. In the *pueblos* (Native American villages) that surround Santa Fe, Christmas is a special time. Here, ceremonies blend Christian practice with tribal traditions. Their echoes are the ancient hymn of this startling land that lies on the high plateaus between snow-covered mountains and the endless western desert.

When Else to Go
September Mild temperatures and plenty of festivities, including the Fiesta de Santa Fe.

PLANNING YOUR TRIP **Getting there**
International flights arrive into Albuquerque, New Mexico, 65 miles (105 km) from Santa Fe. **Getting around** The city is best explored on foot; rent a car if you want to go farther afield. **Weather** Sunny and dry. **Average temperature** 46°F / 7°C.

The buildings on Santa Fe Plaza, illuminated by tiny *farolitos*, twinkling in the night

The Torchlight
Procession marches
down the Royal Mile
to mark the start
of Edinburgh's
Hogmanay

EDINBURGH

Europe Scotland
EDINBURGH

WHY GO *Nights grow darker and colder toward the end of the year, so wrap up warm for a truly memorable party at Edinburgh's Hogmanay.*

At the craggy base of Castle Rock, crowds swell to watch fireworks arc overhead and dazzling rockets rain down through the whiskey-tinged air. Edinburgh is known for many things, but, above all, it's known for Hogmanay, its annual end-of-year, zeitgeist-defining party. This hedonistic three-day curtain raiser to the New Year brings in some 150,000 revelers, all of whom become increasingly animated as the week draws to its climax—midnight on December 31. There's plenty to occupy you during the buildup: concerts, whiskey tastings, bands, DJs, Highland dances, and the Torchlight Procession from the castle to Holyrood Park. It's the greatest New Year celebration on earth, so why not join the party?

When Else to Go
August The Edinburgh Festival Fringe—the largest arts festival in the world—comes to town.

PLANNING YOUR TRIP **Getting there** Edinburgh International Airport has bus and tram links to the city. **Getting around** Buses are reliable, but it is easy to get around on foot. **Weather** Cold, wet, and windy. **Average temperature** 37°F / 3°C.

SYDNEY

Oceania Australia
SYDNEY

WHY GO *Australia's "Harbour City" is the country's party capital, and New Year is the biggest celebration of all. Head to the glittering waterfront to witness the world's most famous fireworks display.*

Sydney is a handsome city set around a sparkling harbor and graced by the impressive Sydney Harbour Bridge. Perhaps most famous is the Opera House, its multipeaked roof evocative of a ship in full sail. A cultural and postmodern metropolis, Sydney has become one of the best places to enjoy New Year's Eve, when the city's waterfront is transformed into a dazzling set piece.

As the light slowly fades on the big day, the harbor fills with twinkling, bobbing boats. Then, at midnight, fireworks erupt from the bridge and light up the sky with eyeball-searing intensity. A curtain of liquid fire drops from the bridge to the water, while volleys of rockets release layer upon layer of colored sheets of flame, a psychedelic starburst of color. When it finishes, it's as though someone has turned the lights out, and the spectators go wild. There's no more Aussie way to celebrate than with a barbecue and a few "tinnies" (cans of beer) at one of the viewpoints. The parties go on till dawn—and beyond.

On New Year's Day, head down to Bondi Beach for a dip in the sea—the perfect remedy for a sore head. If you feel up to it, join locals straddling their surfboards and waiting for the perfect tide. Each big wave's arrival is signaled by a burst of frantic activity, with the successful riding the water into shore. Embrace the brine and start the new year the Aussie way.

When Else to Go
January Events during this month include the Big Bash cricket league and three weeks of arts and culture events for the Sydney Festival.
October The final of the Rugby League, a huge event in the city's calendar.

PLANNING YOUR TRIP **Getting there** Flights arrive into Sydney Airport, 7 miles (12 km) from the city center. **Getting around** The city has an excellent network of buses, light rail, metro, and ferries. Taxis are also cheap. **Weather** Warm weather is virtually guaranteed in December, with cooling sea breezes on the waterfront. **Average temperature** 75°F / 24°C.

Dazzling fireworks exploding over the iconic roof of Sydney Opera House

INDEX

ACKNOWLEDGMENTS

The publisher would like to thank the following for their contributions (in alphabetical order): J.P. Anderson, David Atkinson, Christopher Baker, Pam Barrett, Eleanor Berman, Shawn Blore, Philip Briggs, Christopher Catling, Sue Dobson, Mary Fitzpatrick, Rebecca Ford, Paul Franklin, Aruna Ghose, Jeremy Gray, Paul Greenberg, Eric Grossman, Graeme Harwood, Denise Heywood, Andrew Humphreys, Nick Inman, Yvonne Jeffery, Evelyn Kanter, Christopher Knowles, Tania Kollias, Simon Lewis, Frances Linzee Gordon, Rachel Lovelock, Sinead McGovern, Jenny McKelvie, Robin McKelvie, Mari Nicholson, John Noble, Georgina Palffy, Laura Byrne Paquet, Don Philpott, Eleanor Radford, Nick Rider, Barbara Rodgers, Andrew Sanger, Juergen Scheunemann, Deanna Swaney, Hugh Taylor, Samantha Tidy, Craig Turp, Ross Velton, Joanna Williams, Roger Williams, Helena Zukowski

PICTURE CREDITS

The publisher would like to thank the following for their kind permission to reproduce their photographs:

Key: a-above; b-below/bottom; c-centre; f-far; l-left; r-right; t-top

4Corners: Jordan Banks 162–3; Marco Gaiotti 45bc; Susanne Kremer 154–5, 187bc, 220–21b; Arcangelo Piai 186–7t; Maurizio Rellini 231r; Reinhard Schmid 178b; Anna Serrano 236–7t; Richard Taylor 179t; Francesco Tremolada 36–7.

Alamy Stock Photo: age fotostock 118bc, / Antonio Gravante 93cla; Arco Images GmbH / Arco / F. Schneider 41fcra; Mark Bassett 99br; Paul Brown 74crb; Cavan / Gabe Rogel 15bl; Cosmo Condina 122b; EggImages 185cra; Philip Game 19crb; Jane Gould 41cr; Stephen Harrison 34br; Hemis / Gil Giuglio 225cra, / Escudero Patrick 203l; Justin Hofman 46–7; Bob Hurley 34bl; imageBROKER / Olaf Krüger 232–3, / Moritz Wolf 64clb; Jon Arnold Images Ltd / Michele Falzone 93cl; Scott Kemper 182–3t; Muslianshah Masrie 53tr; mauritius images GmbH / ClickAlps 22cr, / Per-Andre Hoffmann 140–41, / Frank Lukasseck 113tr, / New Zealand Māori Arts and Crafts Institute at Te Puia, Rotorua / Michael Runkel 42br, / Gerhard Wild 237br; Rose-Marie Murray 221tr; National Geographic Image Collection 164–5t, 174–5b, / Chris Bickford 241crb, / Cesare Naldi 22cra; nekphotos 53tc;

Sergi Reboredo 225fcra; robertharding / Kimberly Walker 14; Stocktrek Images, Inc. / Brook Peterson 241cr; Jeremy Sutton-Hibbert 107clb; Nicholas Tinelli 74cra; WaterFrame 175tc; Andrew Wilson 248–9; Jan Wlodarczyk 113br, 192–3; Xinhua / Lu Zhe 85br; ZUMA Press, Inc. 118br.

AWL Images: Peter Adams 171tr; Jon Arnold 24t, 32cr, 32br, 82–3; Aurora Photos 246–7b; Walter Bibikow 247tc; Marco Bottigelli 132–3; Demetrio Carrasco 197bl; Matteo Colombo 112cr; Nigel Pavitt 13tl, 39bc; Doug Pearson 24–5b; Mattes Rene 217bl.

Depositphotos Inc: Baranov_Evgenii 202b.

Dreamstime.com: Andersastphoto 149cr; BarbaraCerovsek 173cr; Jakub Barzycki 40; Lukas Bischoff 196; Thomas Brissiaud 34–5t; Aurora Esperanza Ángeles Flores 130fcra; Markus Gann 43; Georgiakari 78; Helen Hotson 106–7; Tom Meaker 149crb; Glenn Nagel 248b; Cj Nattanai 223br; Sean Pavone 214–15; Peek Creative Collective 101b; Matthew Ragen 74cr; Rosshelen 61br; Alexander Shalamov 175tl; Igor Stevanovic 173cra; Tenkende 93bl; Matthew Train 144–5t; Martin Valigursky 225crb.

Getty Images: 500px / Mikeal Beland 158–9, / Lukas Huber 64cl, / Daniel Kay 98, / Anton Komlev 244cr, / Yash Sheth 52–3b, / Ravi Valdiya 73tc; AFP / Cris Bouroncle 130cra, / Tobias Schwarz 151clb; Steve Allen 225fcr; Arctic-Images 26–7t; artherng 38–9t; Sirachai Arunrugstichai 41fcr; Aurora Photos / Carl D. Walsh 183bc; Adél Békefi 91bl; Walter Bibikow 95t, 234–5; Paul Biris 39bl; Levente Bodo 73tc; Kitti Boonnitrod 16; Boston Red Sox / Billie Weiss 95bl, 95bc; Malcolm P Chapman 219br; Matteo Colombo 60–61, 224–5b; coolbiere photograph 222; Corbis / Jeff Vanuga 153tl; Cultura RM Exclusive / Philip Lee Harvey 244clb; Ian Cumming 58cla, 58r; David Merron Photography 152br; Jeff Diener 27cb; distant lands 12br; Neil Emmerson 65br; Enn Li Photography 183br; EyeEm / Roberto Anania 33, / Cristian Bortes 79bl, / Tom Eversley 107cla, / Till Findl 22br, / Addy Ho 167bc, / Daniel Klatzer 172, / Erlend Krumsvik 73tr, / Scott Puetz 206cr, / Shawn Walters 166–7t; Grant Faint 204–5; Brit Finucci 136–7; fitopardo.com 211clb; National Geographic Image Collection / Chris Schmid 44–5t, / Ralph Lee Hopkins 153r; Geraint Rowland

Photography 211cla; Marc Guitard 13r; Zsolt Hlinka 70–71; Bjorn Holland 76cr; Jeff Hunter 241cra; JKboy Jatenipat 18–19t; John Crux Photography 170–71b, 188bl; Wolfgang Kaehler 108br; Dave G Kelly 64cla; Katja Kreder 76bl; Jonathan Lewis 145br; Vincenzo Lombardo 10bl; David Madison 168–9; Philippe Marion 68br; Matt Anderson Photography 166–7b; Cormac McCreesh 175tr; Buda Mendes 49t; Moment / Luis Dafos 247tr, / Nadya Kulagina 240, / Naomi Rahim 244tr; James Morgan 188–9t; Nature Picture Library / Anup Shah 188bc; Nick Brundle Photography 125br; Ed Norton 88–9; Jake Norton 56bl; Jose Oliveira 6cl; Scott Olson 62–3; PEC Photo 200–201; Juan Pelegrín 6tl; Peter Zelei Images 194–5; Anton Petrus 86–7; Ph. Francesco Ciccotti 176–7; Pixelchrome Inc 76tr; Ratnakorn Piyasirisorost 75; Adrian Pope 30–31; Joe Daniel Price 6b, 96–7, 146–7; Joe Regan 128–9b; robertharding / Oliver Wintzen 69; Michael Roberts 145bl; Ruben Earth 18–19b; SammyVision 54–5; Shestock 104br; shomos uddin 64–5; Simon Phelps Photography 180–81; SinghaphanAllB 28–9, 102–3; VisionsofAmerica / Joe Sohm 142bl; SOPA Images / LightRocket 151br; Kyle Sparks 192b; Alexander Spatari 214–15; SPC#JAYJAY 100–101; Inti St Clair 217br; Stocktrek Images / Yuri Zvezdny 242–3; Murat Taner 48–9b; thipjang 80–81b; David Tipling 27clb; Luca Trovato 92; Pierre Turtaut 231tl; Universal Images Group / Education Images 211cl; VCG 120–21; Simon Watson 199br; Whitworth Images 50–51, 125bc; Terrence wijesena 228–9; Wild Africa Nature 137br; wiratgasem 216–17t; www.christophe faugere.com 10–11t; xia yuan 113tl; Yagi Studio 81tc; Gary Yeowell 198–9; zhangshuang 190–91.

iStockphoto.com: 4X-image 218bl; Orbon Alija 118t; anzeletti 59cra; bluejayphoto 142–3; Britus 163br; calm_eyes 134–5; DanielHarwardt 204bl; E+ / anzeletti 237bc, / borchee 116–17b, 126–7, / DKart 105, / fotoVoyager 156bl, / mbbirdy 20–21, / miralex 19bc, / PeskyMonkey 88bl, / RelaxFoto.de 23, / stockstudioX 56–7, / svetikd 237bl, / TommL 218–19, / zelg 125bl; Em Campos 238–9; fmajor 171tc; Gatsi 110–11; Infografick 148–9b; KenWiedemann 183bl; kokkai 251; lindsay_imagery 55cr; nicomenijes 59br; OSTILL 165bc; Rat0007 113bl; rchphoto 130fbr; RichardALock 55crb; RomaBlack 4–5; Jonathan Ross 66–7; rusm 10bc; simonbradfield 124–5t,

225fbr; Simonology 226–7; Starcevic 206br; Joerg Steber 130fcr; Onur Yuksel 185br; zorazhuang 112tr.

Map by Free Vector Maps http:// freevectormaps.com: 11tc, 12tl, 15ca, 17tl, 18tl, 21tc, 22tl, 24c, 25tl, 26tl, 30tl, 32tl, 35tc, 36tl, 38tl, 41tl, 42tl, 44tl, 47tc, 48tl, 49cr, 52tl, 54tl, 56tl, 57tr, 59tl, 60tl, 62tl, 65tc, 66tl, 68tl, 72tl, 74tl, 77cl, 79tc, 80tl, 82tl, 85cla, 88cra, 89tr, 90tl, 93tc, 94tl, 99tl, 100tl, 101tr, 102tl, 104cla, 107tc, 108tl, 110tl, 112tl, 115tc, 119cla, 120tl, 122tr, 123tr, 124tl, 127tc, 128cla, 130tl, 132tl, 134cla, 136tl, 140tl, 142tr, 143tr, 144tl, 148tl, 150cl, 152tl, 154cla, 157tc, 161cra, 162cla, 163cra, 164tl, 166tl, 169tr, 170cla, 173tl, 174tl, 178ca, 179cr, 181tc, 182tl, 185cla, 186tl, 189ca, 190tl, 192tr, 193tr, 197ca, 199tc, 202cra, 203tr, 205cra, 206tl, 209ca, 211ca, 212ca, 216tl, 219tc, 220tl, 221cr, 223tl, 224tl, 226tl, 229tc, 230tl, 234tl, 236tl, 239tc, 241cla, 242tl, 245cl, 246cla, 248cra, 249tr, 250cla.

Picfair.com: Carlos Sanchez Pereyra 210; Rui Baiao 130crb; Stockimo 156–7; John Such 184.

Robert Harding Picture Library: Neale Clark 128–9t; Frans Lanting 164–5b.

Shutterstock: aodaodaodaod 55cra; Eric Valenne geostory 149cra; Seljan Gurbanova 173crb; Ric Jacyno 129bc; nicolasvoisin44 41crb; Soonthorn Wongsaita 41fbr.

SuperStock: age fotostock / Toño Labra 85cra.

Unsplash: Alexandra Andersson 104crb; Mar Cerdeira 151t; Drew Colins 207; Kylie Docherty 90–91t; Michael Durana 208–9; elCarito / Wild Drawing Believe in Dreams 91br; Yuriy Garnaev 72–3; Drew Hays 122–3; Braden Jarvis 212–13; Valentin B. Kremer 187tr; L A L A 132br; Tim Marshall 42crb; Joshua Medway 39br; Random Institute 44–5b; Jailam Rashad 8–9; Hans Reniers 91bc; Heather Shevlin 2; Shounen21 109; Sorasak 6tr; Match Sùmàyà 81tr; Willian Justen de Vasconcellos 131; William Warby 186–7b; Sander Wehkamp 160–61; Fatih Yürür 84.

Cover images:
Front and Back: **Unsplash:** Simon Matzinger.

For further information see: www.dkimages.com